Debatable Humor

Debatable Humor

Laughing Matters on the 2008 Presidential Primary Campaign

Patrick A. Stewart

LEXINGTON BOOKS
Lanham • Boulder • New York • Toronto • Plymouth, UK

Published by Lexington Books
A wholly owned subsidiary of The Rowman & Littlefield Publishing Group, Inc.
4501 Forbes Boulevard, Suite 200, Lanham, Maryland 20706
www.rowman.com

10 Thornbury Road, Plymouth PL6 7PP, United Kingdom

British Library Cataloguing in Publication Information Available

Library of Congress Cataloging-in-Publication Data

Stewart, Patrick A., 1966–
  Debatable humor : laughing matters on the 2008 presidential primary campaign / Patrick
A. Stewart.
    p. cm.
  Includes index.
  ISBN 978-0-7391-6696-3 (cloth : alk. paper)—ISBN 978-0-7391-6697-0 (pbk. : alk.
paper)—ISBN 978-0-7391-7414-2 (ebook)
  1. Presidents—United States—Election—2008. 2. Wit and humor—Political aspects—
United States. I. Title.
  JK5262008 .S87 2012
  324.973'0931—dc23

                                                      2012001250

♾™ The paper used in this publication meets the minimum requirements of American
National Standard for Information Sciences—Permanence of Paper for Printed Library
Materials, ANSI/NISO Z39.48-1992.

Printed in the United States of America

To my life's love
Jennifer
Whose gift of joyous laughter
Replenishes and renews me

Contents

Acknowledgements

This being my first book, there are almost too many people to thank for assisting me on my path to this point. Sharp eyes that have edited this book, and the work that led to it, tightening my prose, expanding my mind, and refining my arguments include Larry Arnhart, Lara Brown, Erik Bucy, Andrew Dowdle, Thomas Flamson, Brett Himmler, Michael Krasner, Roger Masters, Marc Mehu, Tracey Platt, Matthew Ramsey, Frank Salter, and the unnamed reviewers at the journals *Humor: International Journal of Humor*, with chapter 4 based on the forthcoming article "Laughter on the campaign trail: How 2008 presidential candidates used humor during primary debates," and *Politics and the Life Sciences*, with chapter 5 derived from "Presidential laugh lines: Candidate display behavior and audience laughter in the 2008 primary elections," 29(2), 55-72 (September 2010). I would also like to thank all those who commented on earlier drafts of chapters at the *International Society for Human Ethology* (ISHE), as well as for welcoming me into the field of human ethology, including Tom Alley, Maryanne Fisher, Daniel Kruger, Peter LaFreniere, Elisabeth Oberzaucher, Wulf Schiefenhövel, and Glenn Weisfeld; in addition I would like to thank Frank Salter and Marina Vancatova of Charles University in Prague, Czech Republic, for inviting me to present at their Human Ethology Summer School in 2010, although the Icelandic volcano made me personally unavailable, being able to present using technology provided me the opportunity to distill my thoughts. And while he was not able to continue with me on the ethological path, Mike Cundall's philosopher's insights incited my initial interest and research.

I would also like to thank the graduate students whose data collection and editorial assistance have been invaluable and irreplaceable. These students include Ryan Robeson and Craig Teague from Arkansas State University and Karen Sebold, Lauren Merritt, Amber Kandur, and Ann Diallo from the University of Arkansas. Ryan and Craig were invaluable in providing inter-coder reliability on the nonverbal data used throughout the book, whereas Karen, Amber and Ann did an excellent job in providing data on Federal Election Commission (FEC) and media coverage used in chapter 3. Finally, Lauren provided final editorial support on short notice, for which I am quite grateful. Without their support and hard labor, this book would not be nearly so rigorous and insightful. Furthermore, the continuous editorial support of Joe Parry (now moved on to greater things), Melissa Wilks, Allison Northridge, and Lindsey Schauer of Lexington Press has provided me a stable basis to build from, and provided me assistance when I needed it most.

Scholarship builds upon the work, insight, and support of great teachers and mentors: I have benefitted greatly throughout my academic career by some incredible individuals willing to invest their time and energies in what probably seemed like a long-shot. The professors and mentors whose countless hours of (mostly) unrewarded assistance helped shape me as a scholar while exemplifying a playful curiosity about the world and how to explore it include Ann Sorensen, Andrea Bonnicksen, James Schubert, Henry Kennedy, and countless others whose classes I have taken and learned from in my path from St. Petersburg Junior College, to the University of Central Florida, and finally to my Ph.D. studies at Northern Illinois University.

Likewise, my colleagues and friends in the *Association for Politics and the Life Sciences* (APLS) have provided a home for creativity and risk-taking with their willingness to entertain ideas and theories that cross academic boundaries that has served my curiosity well since I joined the association as a new Ph.D. student at Northern Illinois University in 1992. Not only did I benefit from the incredible scholars in the Political Science and Public Administration programs there, by housing the only *Politics and the Life Sciences* Ph.D. program in the world, NIU's leadership and risk taking allowed me to take a path few others would have the opportunity to tread.

In the most applied sense, I would like to thank the Arkansas State University Rugby Football Club. For nine years I had the distinct joy of associating with the finest of young men in this most rough-and-tumble of all sports while working at ASU. Being on faculty at ASU allowed me to pursue my passion of rugby, and it was here that for nearly a decade playing the role of assistant coach and "first follower" to head coach Curt Huckaby I learned the importance of laughter and humor for successful leadership, winning one national championship and (perhaps more pertinently) losing three championship games. Even from afar, with my coaching days well behind me, watching this elite program increasing success at the highest level gives me great pride as the current head coach, and my ex-graduate assistant, Matt Huckaby, has blossomed into an acclaimed and elite university rugby coach, recognized as amongst the best in the United States, by marrying a keen intellect and fervent work ethic with a playfulness that brings out the best in his players.

Additionally, I would like to thank Dr. Peter S. Ruckman for his complicity in our comedy-driven shenanigans; without his dry wit and ethanol-sourced research, I would not be the political scientist I am today, nor would I have publications in both the fields of alcohol policy and political science wit.

Penultimately, I would like to thank my family. Besides being the love of my life and the source of more joy and laughter than I could possibly deserve, my wife Jennifer has been my most ardent supporter, vigilant editor and definitive intellectual touchstone. For that alone, her parents Jack and Jeannie Majors deserve my highest thanks; but more than that they have given me a home and family in the heart of America. Further, my sisters Launa, Lisa and Laura have all had a hand in shaping my humor (as siblings invariably do!) and have been a source of great pride for me over the years, while my parents Gail and Wayne have taught me the importance of humor and laughter in forming resilience.

And finally, I want to thank the University of Arkansas for providing a nurturing, supportive environment. From the chancellor to my colleagues in the Department of Political Science, I feel honored to be a part of a workplace that values all participants in the education process, and most of all, for making work seem like just so much play—which fortunately it is!

Chapter 1
Laughing Matters on the Campaign Trail: Humor and Laughter in the 2008 Presidential Primary Debates

The 2008 presidential election was a historical campaign not just due to the groundbreaking front-running candidacies of Hillary Clinton, Barack Obama, Mitt Romney, and John McCain, who represented the first serious front-running candidates based upon sex, race, religion, and age, respectively, but also due to the sheer numbers of contending candidates. For the first time since 1928, both political parties' primaries were wide open affairs with no incumbent or vice president running; indeed, by the tenor of the debates the incumbent administration of George W. Bush appeared unpopular with both parties. In total, eight Democratic Party and ten Republican Party candidates left the primary starting gates by taking part in early-spring and late-summer debates. By the time the candidates entered the home stretch of primary voting that started in New Hampshire, five Republican and five Democratic Party candidates had fallen by the wayside. And by the time the Super Tuesday results were posted and digested, the electoral field for both political parties had narrowed even further to just Clinton and Obama for the Democratic Party and McCain, Mike Huckabee and Ron Paul on the Republican side.

Although paid media and in-person campaigning pays dividends to candidates willing to invest time and energy, the ability of the candidates to set themselves apart from the other candidates, especially in a crowded field such as in 2008, is of great importance for electoral survival and, ultimately, success.

Nowhere is the importance of presidential candidate self-presentation, and the concomitant use of laughter-eliciting humor, more apparent than in political debates. This is despite the fact that presidential debates are high stakes events in which verbal and nonverbal miscues have the potential to obscure successful performances. Such "defining moments" become the most memorable aspect of a candidate's debate performance [1] and may change the course of a campaign in a single relatable instant.[2] One such defining moment occurred in 1976 when President Gerald Ford, meeting challenger Jimmy Carter in their second debate, made what appeared to be an innocuous comment concerning Eastern European nations and their not being under the domination of the Soviet Union. His response was a source of extensive media criticism concerning his knowledge of national security issues, which was seen as one of his strong points, in turn leading to public opinion turning away from him in the days leading up to his electoral defeat. Therefore, as can be expected, campaigns attempt to insulate their candidate from unscripted, unexpected, and (presumably) unwanted "defining moments" by negotiating the format, number and timing of debates.[1] This has reduced debates from free-flowing interactive events to what has been referred to as "side-by-side press conferences" [3, 4] in which as much control over the substance and style of candidate utterances is exerted.

However, debates are venues in which candidates may directly communicate with the voters, one in which there is a magnified sense of intimacy with viewers having the illusion of inviting candidates into their home for a discussion over policy and politics.[5] Even in less-than-compelling elections, citizens value debates for their ability to directly provide information about the candidates, information that may supersede other sources in influencing voters due to it being unmediated by press interpretation or campaign spin.[4] Candidates are thus rewarded for engaging in relational communication that focuses on informal and friendly interpersonal eloquence while avoiding the appearance of formality and detachment.[5, 6, a] As noted by Pfau & Rang: "*candidates who seek to enhance their persuasiveness in televised political debates should use relational messages that feature more similarity and involvement and, to a lesser degree, more composure*" (p. 124; italics theirs).

Therefore, while candidates jockey for public attention and support in the competitive venue of debates that highlights strengths and exposes weaknesses, they have an incentive to develop a connection with potential voters. A well-delivered quip can signal shared values,[7] solidify a candidate's likability, and may even turn a debate (and campaign) around. A classic example is that of President Ronald Reagan responding to concerns over his advanced age and leadership competency that became prominent after a faltering performance during his first debate with Minnesota Senator Walter Mondale. By retorting "I will not make age an issue of this campaign. I am not going to exploit, for political purposes, my opponent's youth and inexperience," Reagan not only inoculated himself from future age-related concerns by highlighting his cleverness and ability to connect with the audience, but also appeared to put Senator Mondale and the moderator off stride, with Mondale smiling broadly and the moderator Henry Trewhitt commenting about Reagan "I'd like to head for the fence and try to catch that one before it goes over."[8] With this defining moment, Reagan was able to reinvigorate his public persona and recapture the presidency.[1]

Prior research concerning politician humor

This book most likely represents the first systematic quantitative analysis of the use of humor by politicians on the campaign trail. Specifically, this book considers how humor is used in primary debates, and how the resultant laughter (indicating successful humor) may have an influence on electoral outcomes. Additionally, it considers how the humor used and the laughter that follows reflects the underlying power relationships, political norms, and personalities of the candidates and their political parties. In sum, humor can tell us more than just that which is "funny"; it can provide a "thin-slice" perspective of the political arena and the politicians that inhabit it.[9]

While there has been a proliferation of research concerning the effect of humor in the mass media on attitudes towards politicians and political participation, with Baumgartner and Morris' edited volume "Laughing Matters: Humor and American Politics in the Media Age"[10] and Gray, Jones and Thompson's "Satire TV: Politics and Comedy in the Post-Network Era"[11] being prime collections of research considering the role of humor on the political landscape in the United States, little research has considered the humor of political candidates.[b] Specifically, despite our living in an era dominated by video on demand and videos on the Internet, little systematic investigation has considered the influence of humor generated by the politicians themselves, especially when they are on the campaign trail.

What research considering politician humor that does exist tends to be of a descriptive and/or theoretical nature, relying more on anecdotal accounts than systematic collection and analysis. For instance, President Gerald Ford's "Humor and the Presidency,"[12] Arizona Senator and 1976 Democratic Party presidential candidate Morris K. Udall's "Too Funny to be President,"[13] and Kansas Senator and 1996 Republican Party presidential candidate Bob Dole's "Great Political Wit: Laughing (Almost) All the Way to the White House"[14] provide an insider's perspective on the use and importance of humor, as Ford, Udall, and Dole regale readers with their recollections both as politicians on the campaign trail and as elected public servants. These books provide examples of jokes that work(ed) for themselves and other politicians and lessons learned, in terms of practical application. Udall, in particular, provides common sense advice such as recycling good jokes, practicing phrasing, delivering and timing, knowing your audience, being topical, being self-deprecatory, and avoiding racist, ethnic and sexist jokes (pp. 191-199). At the same time, these books may be seen as a justification for political careers that did not reach the expected pinnacles. Specifically, Gerald Ford was a President immortalized by the political satire of Chevy Chase on the groundbreaking humor show Saturday Night Live, which in turn defined/maligned the then President as clumsy and not the most intellectually capable individual; at the same time Ford appreciated the importance of humor enough to hire a campaign writer exclusively devoted to producing jokes. In the case of Morris Udall, his book provides a rationale of sorts for not ascending to the highest office of the land despite a successful and storied career as a civil servant, and thus provides an opportunity to revisit his "greatest hits" as a political functionary.[c] Likewise, Bob Dole's book can be read as a rejoinder to those who found out he "wasn't the glowering, Social Security-devouring sourpuss they'd come to know, if not to like, from watching all those attack ads made possible by White House coffee drinkers" (p. xii).

Books taking a broader perspective, considering candidate use of political humor during presidential campaigns and by Presidents while in the White House include Gerald Gardner's "Campaign Comedy: Political Humor from

Clinton to Kennedy"[15] and Arthur Sloane's "Humor in the White House: The Wit of Five American Presidents."[16] Both of these books provide a journalistic-style descriptive foray into general election and governing humor which focuses on successful and memorable witticisms. Gardner, a film and television writer who won an Emmy for his political satire, takes a look at nine presidential campaigns in which televised media brought the humor of candidates directly to the voters by considering how each candidate used, or didn't use, humor during the course of their election. Sloane's book takes a look at the five presidents most known for their humor, Abraham Lincoln, Calvin Coolidge, Franklin D. Roosevelt, John F. Kennedy, and Ronald Reagan, considering the source of their humor from a more academic, yet still descriptive, style.

While these four books provide insight into the personal styles of select politicians, and practical advice concerning the presentation of humor, they do little to provide a systematic understanding of why humor works, and how it affects electoral outcomes. From these books we learn that while the candidates, especially those known for their charisma, had strong senses of humor that reflected their personal world-view and often shined-forth in their interactions with the press and the public, this humor was often augmented by speechwriters who provided quips and anecdotes before many of the candidates' public appearances. For instance, Sloane[16] notes that speechwriter and humor consultant Landon Parvin put together from three to six pages of self-deprecatory comments for Ronald Reagan before each of his speeches that played to the much-beloved President's sense of humor and sunny disposition (p. 184). On the other hand, despite being known for his expansive smile, Jimmy Carter had an acerbic wit that led to him sarcastically attacking supporters. As related by Gardner[15], a senior Carter aide noted "Jimmy's idea of self-deprecating humor is to insult his staff" (p. 137). In sum, these books appear to indicate that humor provides a "thin-slice" insight into the candidates and their personalities not only through their self-generated humor, but also their choice of and decision to use (or not) humor generated by professional speechwriters and consultants.

Two books analyzing political humor stand out by attempting to find a theoretical basis for humor and then considering its application in light of this. Charles E. Schutz's "Political Humor: From Aristophanes to Sam Ervin"[17] provides an attempt to understand humor by political leaders and its role in governing ranging in time from classical Athenian democracy to Watergate era United States. Although Schutz does extremely well with providing a political philosopher's perspective from Abraham Lincoln to the mid-1970s, he excels in tracing political humor to its roots in ancient Athens where the plays of Aristophanes and the philosophy of Socrates, as related by Plato, are mined for its political satire. Here, Schutz portrays humor as paralleling democratic politics by "sublimating man's aggressions into peaceful wordplay" (p. 14).

More recently, Dean L. Yarwood engaged in a systematic analysis of the use of humor in the U.S. Congress[18] both through textual analysis and interviews of past and present representatives, considering its effect on working relationships. Yarwood's analysis of the use of humor to both enforce and challenge norms in this elite policy making body provides the most recent, practical and scientifically compelling treatment of the constant, yet ever variable nature of political humor. However, by focusing on the role humor plays as a social lubricant in a closed club, this book avoids focusing attention on how humor conveys a politician's style and personality to the voting public through the lens of the media. Therefore, although these books provide useful insights into the nature of humor, both in governing and on the campaign trail, they likewise reveal unaddressed research questions deriving from the data being analyzed.

Humor theory and evolutionary approaches

The study of humor has a long and illustrious history, tracing itself back to ancient Greece. Here, the "superiority" theory of humor, in which the purpose of humor is to elevate oneself at the expense of others, inception is attributed to Plato, Aristotle, and, more recently Thomas Hobbes. More recently, the "relief" theory of humor, in which laughter is seen as the release of excess nervous energy, can be attributed to Herbert Spencer and Sigmund Freud, whereas "incongruity" theory, in which the humorousness of a comment is derived from the unexpectedness of the punchline, can be seen as a result of more cognitivist appreciation of humor.[18-19] Despite the extensive amount of research and intellectual ruminations concerning humor, its sources and the purpose it is put to, there is a distinct lack of a unified approach that allows for objective coding scheme due to the overlapping nature of these theories.

As can be expected, humor is a notoriously difficult concept to define. John Morreal's recent work[20] provides a basic pattern for humor: 1) a rapid cognitive shift in thoughts and/or perceptions; 2) engagement in a "play" mode in which there is disengagement from conceptual and practical concerns; 3) enjoyment of this cognitive shift; and 4) signaling pleasure through laughter (p. 50). While laughter is easily observed, and may be seen as the preferred endpoint of humorous comments, and nonverbal displays may indicate intent, humorous comments can be decomposed in multiple different ways to extract meaning. While the major target of comments are nearly always obvious, what might appear to target one individual or group may very well have implied attacks for another group. Humor also depends upon shared perceptions and implied messages relying upon contextual understanding. These encrypted aspects of humor, which are not necessarily recognized by the general population and may be best appreciated by a subset of those "in the know," may add to the enjoyment of humor.[7] Therefore, besides the very basic attributes of humor, such as the primary target of such comments, humor leaves much knowledge to be mined.

Understanding what drives this may be best approached through evolutionary perspectives. Recent research suggests laughter predates speech, and indeed might be a precursor to speech, and serves to coordinate group activities to assist in survival of related individuals. Therefore, due to the survival potential afforded by humor,[21-22] evolutionary perspectives are pursued in this book due to both their explanatory power, and their cohesiveness in comparison with the range of humor theories available. However, due to the range of evolutionary mechanisms at play with both laughter and humor,[23] this book is grounded in evolutionary theory, but does not purport to directly test the various theories in use.

Dissecting political humor[d]

The lack of systematic analysis of humor by politicians is understandable given the complexity such an endeavor presents. Specifically, while humor has a very strong cognitive element, mainly through the playful use of words to introduce or underline incongruity, it also has a very strong emotion-based component. Furthermore, humor is arguably not successful unless there is laughter, a physio-logical and, some might claim, emotional response.[21, 24] Here laughter, whether it derives from individuals on the panel or the audience as a whole, provides the defining test for humor. Specifically, humor in this study is defined by the laughter that follows—this, however, does not mean that humor is reliant on laughter for its definition. However, for the sake of measurement validity, in the work presented here laughter defines humor. In addition to laughter, other non-verbal cues play a role in how humorous a comment is perceived. Specifically, punch-line cues by the "joke-teller" using the face and the body have long been recognized as playing a significant role in how humorous a comment is per-ceived by the audience, as shall be discussed in chapter 5.

Figure 1.1: Average number of humorous comments * debate season

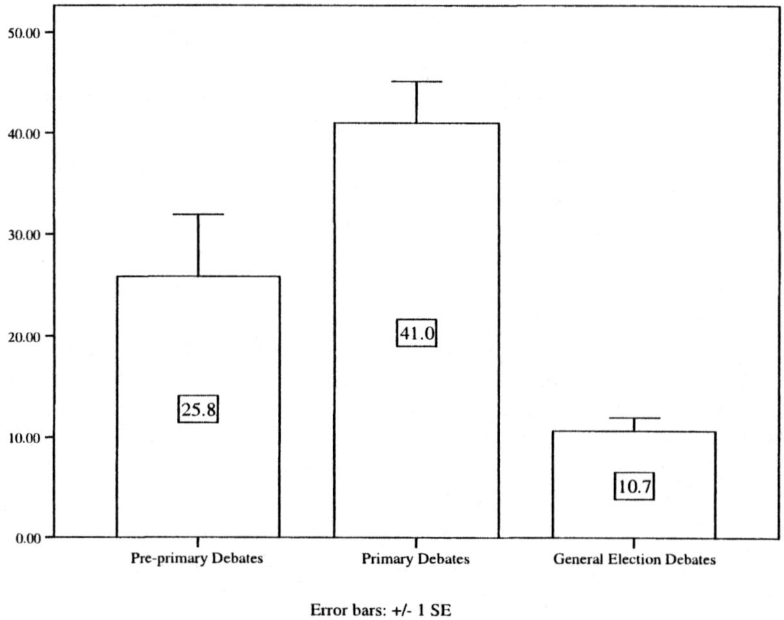

Error bars: +/- 1 SE

Humor also plays an important role in communicating and affecting status, with successful "joke-tellers" (defined by audience laughter) both more likely to be liked before they tell a joke, but also more likely to be liked more as a result of successfully telling a joke.[25] Therefore, while debates and speeches by politicians are not "joke-telling" contests, humor is an important part of self-definition in the competition for attention and the status that derives from that attention. However, not all debates are the same. Primary debates can be considered "hot-beds" of humor in comparison with general election debates. Specifically, the in-group primary debates aren't as deadly serious as between-group debates of the general election, especially as audiences appear to be more likely to laugh when surrounded by like-minded individuals. As can be seen in Figure 1.1, the average number of humorous comments both early in the primary season during the first three debates given by both political parties and immediately before the New Hampshire and Super Tuesday primaries are much higher than that during the three general election presidential debates during the 2008 electoral season.

At the same time, the humor used can be "other-deprecatory," in other words humor in which the joke told attacks and derogates competition, both from within the cast of competitors or an opposition party; humorous comments may also be used to make fun of the speaker him/herself. In this latter case, self-deprecatory humor can humanize candidates by showing they are "like everyone else" despite their elevated status, as they lower themselves to be laughed at and with. However, with this "self-deprecatory" humor in which the target of the joke is the teller him or herself, the candidate must have a high enough level of prestige to be able to "give" some of it away in a joke.

Finally, context plays a role in the reception of humor coming from the candidates. A factor that became quite apparent was that audience laughter was much easier to elicit during primary debates than during the general election debates. While John McCain and Barack Obama both elicited more than their fair share of laughter during the nearly two-year long electoral campaign, the amount and intensity of laughter diminished radically from when they performed in front of partisan audiences during the primaries to when they debated against each other in front of independent or mixed political party audiences. Quips that worked in front of partisan audiences did not necessarily work in front of mixed party or independent audiences. For instance, Barack Obama's commenting "Senator McCain, I think the straight talk express lost a wheel on that one," during the Nashville general election debate, reprising a laughter-eliciting line he used during the Democratic Party Super Tuesday debate when he commented to "And somewhere along the line the straight talk express lost some wheels" did not lead to audience laughter. Whether this is due to the candidates' humorous comments being oversubscribed to by their use in prior debates and speeches, instructions to the audience by moderators to hold their applause until after the debate was over, the diminished power of emotional contagion in mixed audiences, the greater gravity of the presidential debates, or a combination of these factors, the difference in amount and intensity of laughter was marked. Therefore, primary debates provide the most fruitful venue for analyzing humor and laughter due to the amount and variability of "humor events" not available during the general election debates, although the lessons learned can be applied regardless of venue.

While this book might not be able to address all the questions raised about who elicited laughter and how they elicited it, as well as the precise impact of humor and laughter on the electoral process, it attempts to take an important first step towards understanding the substance and importance of humor and the laughter it elicits. To do so, the historical 2008 presidential primaries of both political parties are considered. The first three debates for both the Republican and Democratic parties provide a baseline before expectations were set and front-runners decided, whereas the debates prior to the New Hampshire and Super Tuesday primaries were held when the front-runners were well-defined despite the races still being unsettled, as neither party had decided on their presidential candidate (see Box 1.1).

Observing and analyzing political behavior

With the understanding that observing and measuring human behavior is a necessary first step towards understanding, in other words, as succinctly stated by Nico Tinbergen[26] "contempt for simple observation is a lethal trait in any science" (p. 412), this book draws upon observation of laughter and the events that cause it. Although there are limitations with observational research, as with any research method, the design used here addresses multiple concerns that may be raised. Most importantly, the effect of observing behavior does not pose a concern, especially as we are interested in politician performance in the naturalistic environment of debates.

With this in mind, the structure of the book is as follows: in the next chapter, I consider how humor, especially that deriving from candidates during primary debates, might influence the outcome of presidential elections. To do so, I use a theoretical perspective that arises from both economics and evolutionary biology: signaling theory. Specifically, I consider how both laughter and humor function as social signals with laughter serving as a signal of social sustenance for the producer of the humor, and the humor serving as a "thin-slice" of the speaker's intelligence, personality, and values,[9] as well as an index of the candidate's connection with their audience.[27] I next consider the role humor and concomitant laughter might play in signaling candidate quality and support to voters, namely the effect of self- and other-deprecatory humorous comments. I also consider a broader perspective concerning the role humor plays in political systems both as reflecting the social and political values of contending parties, as well as the values held by the system in general.

The third chapter considers the influence humor and resultant laughter during debates has outside the debate arena. Specifically, I posit that the candidate who uses humor effectively to elicit audience support through laughter can be expected to influence the level of support a candidate receives in terms of media coverage and fundraising. Specifically, I expect that candidates who make humorous comments during political debates will be more likely to obtain precious media coverage and raise more money from greater numbers of individuals, especially in the early debates prior to the establishment of front-runners. The question remains as to whether it is the sheer number of humorous comments, the audience's response, or whether other factors are at play.

The following chapter considers who elicits laughter and the target of the humor comment, both in terms of political party and the tier of the candidate. The influence of political party on both the generation, audience response to and target of humorous comments may be seen in the norms concerning the maintenance of group boundaries. In other words, humor may be seen as a form of aggression towards those individuals and groups that are threats to the social values held by the political party of the audience and humorous comment maker. Candidate tier likewise plays an important role in both audience reception of humor, willingness to attempt humor and the target of that humor, as frontrunners and second-tier candidates will use different humor strategies.

The fifth chapter focuses on the nonverbal cues used by the maker of humorous comments considering whether there are definite facial display patterns associated with audience laughter. Specifically, we consider whether there are facial displays present, and if so, whether there are differences based upon the target of the comment, and whether the displays correlate with who laughs and how hard they laugh. Here we consider whether different types of smiles, whether "felt," "false," or "fear," have an impact on who laughs, as well as how hard the audience is judged to laugh.

The sixth and last substantive chapter takes an in-depth look at the humor styles of individual candidates focusing on Barack Obama and Hilary Clinton of the Democratic Party and John McCain and Mike Huckabee of the Republican Party. Here, a qualitative analysis of candidate utterances is carried out, considering the nature of the humor used, whether jokes or witticisms, the target of the jokes, whether self- or other-deprecatory, as well as the different types of nonverbal cues that accompanied their humor is used. In addition, I consider how the target of this humor responded, if present and within view of the cameras. In this chapter, inferences are drawn concerning the political norms and personality characteristics signaled by the humor used.

This final chapter draws conclusions concerning humor and laughter. Both practical applications and theoretical insights may be derived from the research carried out, with suggestions for both candidates and their staffs on the campaign trail and for academics considering future research directions. One finding stands out: the use of humor in debates suggest debate performance is less about scoring points with well-reasoned arguments (although this is important and noted in its absence) and more about developing personal connections with the audience, whether in the building or at home.

The 2008 Presidential Primary Debates
The first Republican presidential debate was held at the Ronald Reagan Presidential Library in Simi Valley, California, on 3 May 2007 and ran for 90 minutes. Beginning at 8 p.m. (EDT), it was broadcast on both MSNBC and politico.com with Chris Matthews the primary moderator. The second Republican debate was held on 15 May 2007 on the campus of the University of South Carolina in Columbia. The debate began at 8 p.m. (EDT) and ran for 90 minutes. It aired on Fox News with Brit Hume the primary moderator. The third Republican debate was on 5 June 2007 at Saint Anselm College in Manchester, New Hampshire. The debate aired from 7 p.m. to 9 p.m. (EDT) and could be seen on CNN and the CNN website. The debate was moderated by Wolf Blitzer. In these three debates, a full field of ten candidates appeared including: Sam Brownback, Mike Huckabee, Duncan Hunter, Jim Gilmore, Rudy Giuliani, John McCain, Ron Paul, Mitt Romney, Tom Tancredo, and Tommy Thompson.

The first Democratic presidential debate was held at South Carolina State University in Orangeburg, South Carolina. It was held on 26 April 2007, making it the first debate for either party, and was aired on MSNBC from 7:00-8:30 p.m. (EDT). The debate was moderated by Brian Williams with questions from the general public. The second Democratic debate was held in Manchester, New Hampshire, on 3 June 2007 at Saint Anselm College and moderated by Wolf Blitzer. The debate aired on CNN from 7-9 p.m. (EDT). The third Democratic debate was held 28 June 2007 in Washington, DC. The event was organized by PBS and was held on the Howard University campus. The debate lasted 90 minutes, beginning at 9 p.m. (EDT), and was moderated by Tavis Smiley. Questions came from various sources including a panel of distinguished persons and were fielded by Hillary Clinton, Joe Biden, Christopher Dodd, John Edwards, Mike Gravel, Dennis Kucinich, Barack Obama, and Bill Richardson.

The final debates were chosen based upon their proximity in time to two key primaries, New Hampshire and Super Tuesday. In recognition of the New Hampshire primary being the first primary of the electoral season, ABC hosted back-to-back primary debates of Republican, then Democratic Party candidates on 5 January 2008. This event was held in Manchester, New Hampshire, was moderated by Charles Gibson and featured a diminished field of candidates, with the Republican field reduced to six candidates: Huckabee, Guiliani, McCain, Paul, Romney, and Fred Thompson. The Democratic Party likewise saw a sharp reduction in the numbers of their candidates, with only front-runners Clinton, Edwards, and Obama participating in the debate.

Super Tuesday involved 24 states and one territory in primaries and caucuses and was considered the most important of electoral dates. As such, CNN hosted Republican and Democratic debates on back-to-back nights of January 30 and 31. The first debate, the Republican debate, was held in Simi Valley, California, was moderated by Anderson Cooper and saw a Republican field reduced to four candidates: Huckabee, McCain, Paul and Romney. The next night, the Democratic Party debate was held in Hollywood, California, was moderated by Wolf Blitzer and saw Hillary Clinton and Barack Obama spar.

Notes

[a] One of the reasons given for Richard M. Nixon losing his historic first debate with John F. Kennedy was his formal bearing, which stood in sharp contrast with Kennedy's informal, relationally intimate performance.

[b] Exceptions to this include experimental work by Robert Priest[28-29] nearly forty years ago, as well as recent endeavors by Amy Bippus.[30] However, while this work is quite useful for understanding humor and what drives our perceptions of it, does not focus on analyzing the use of humor by politicians in the field.

[c] Ironically, Udall's message echoes that of Senator Thomas Corwin's advice to President Garfield a century earlier, known as Corwin's law of American politics and recounted by Schutz[17]: "Never make people laugh. If you would succeed in life, you must be solemn, solemn as an ass. All great monuments are built over solemn asses" (p. 24). Corwin, like Udall, was known for his artful skill as a political humorist-practitioner; however, as noted by Yarwood[18] Corwin was afraid his legacy would be solely that as a "clown" (p. 25, 30).

[d] With all due respect to Gerald Gardner[15] who comments "The dissection of humor is not a promising enterprise. It is not unlike the dissection of a frog in a high school science lab. The student is permitted to take a close look at the innards of the frog, but what has he learned? Dissecting political humor is equally unproductive, and so this book will not attempt it" (p. 14). I take out the scalpel to understand what is arguably an understudied yet highly important aspect of politics.

References

1. Zakahi, W. R. & Hacker, K. L. in *Candidate Images in Presidential Elections* (ed Hacker, K. E.) 99-122 (Praeger, Westport, CT, 1995).
2. Gentry, W. A. & Duke, M. P. A historical perspective on nonverbal communication in debates: Implications for elections and leadership. *Journal of Leadership Studies 2*, 36-47 (2009).
3. Lanoue, D. J. & Schrott, P. R. in *The Joint Press Conference: The history, impact, and prospects of American presidential debates* 173 (Greenwood Press, Westport, CT, 1991).
4. Lemert, J. B., Elliott, W. R., Bernstein, J. M., Rosenberg, W. L. & Nestvold, K. J. in *News verdicts, the debates, and presidential campaigns* (Praeger Press, Westport, CT, 1991).
5. Pfau, M. & Rang, J. G. The impact of relational messages on candidate influence in televised political debates. *Communication Studies 42*, 114-128 (1991).
6. Husson, W., Stephen, T., Harrison, T. & Fehr, B. J. An interpersonal communication perspective on images of political candidates. *Human communication research 14*, 397-421 (1988).

8. Fein, S., Goethals, G. R. & Kugler, M. B. Social Influence on Political Judgments: The Case of Presidential Debates. *Polit. Psychol. 28*, 165-192 (2007).
9. Borkenau, P., Mauer, N., Riemann, R., Spinath, F. M. & Angleitner, A. Thin slices of behavior as cues of personality and intelligence. *J. Pers. Soc. Psychol. 86*, 599-614 (2004).
10. Baumgartner, J. C., Ed, & Morris, J. S., Ed., in *Laughing matters humor and American politics in the media age* (Routledge, New York; London, 2008).
11. Gray, J., Jones, J. P. & Thompson, E. in *Satire TV: Politics and comedy in the post-network era* 283 (New York University Press, New York, 2009).
12. Ford, G. R. in *Humor and the Presidency* 162 (Arbor House, New York, 1987).
13. Udall, M. K. in *Too funny to be President* 249 (The University of Arizona Press, Tucson, AZ, 1988).
14. Dole, B. in *Great political wit: Laughing (almost) all the way to the White House* 203 (Broadway, New York: NY, 2000).
15. Gardner, G., & Gardner, G. Mocking of the president, in *Campaign comedy: political humor from Clinton to Kennedy* (Wayne State University Press, Detroit, 1994).
16. Sloane, A. A. in *Humor in the White House: the wit of five American presidents* 208 (McFarland & Co Inc Pub, Jefferson, NC, 2001).
17. Schutz, C. E. in *Political humor: from Aristophanes to Sam Ervin* (Fairleigh Dickinson University Press, Rutherford NJ, 1977).
18. Yarwood, D. L. in *When Congress makes a joke: Congressional humor then and now* 161 (Rowman & Littlefield Publishers, Inc., Lanham, MD, 2004).
19. Martin, R. A. in *The psychology of humor: An integrative approach* (Elsevier, Amsterdam, Netherlands, 2007).
20. Morreall, J. in *Comic relief: A comprehensive philosophy of humor* 187 (Wiley-Blackwell, Malden, MA, 2009).
21. Panksepp, J. in *Affective neuroscience: the foundations of human and animal emotions* 466 (Oxford University Press, New York, 1998).
22. Panksepp, J. Neuroevolutionary sources of laughter and social joy: Modeling primal human laughter in laboratory rats. *Behav. Brain Res. 182*, 231-244 (2007).
23. Gervais, M. & Wilson, D. S. The evolution and functions of laughter and humor: a synthetic approach. *Q. Rev. Biol. 80*, 395-430 (2005).
24. Provine, R. R. in *Laughter: A scientific investigation* (Penguin Press, New York, NY, 2001).
25. Stewart, P. A. The influence of self- and other-deprecatory humor on presidential candidate evaluation during the 2008 election. *Social Science Information 50*, 201-222 (2011).
26. Tinbergen, N. On aims and methods of ethology. *Zeitschrift für Tierpsychologie 20*, 410-433 (1963).

27. Maynard-Smith, J. & Harper, D. in *Animal signals* (Oxford Univ. Press, New York, NY, 2003).
28. Priest, R. F. Election jokes: The effects of reference group membership. *Psychol. Rep. 18*, 600-602 (1966).
29. Priest, R. F. & Abrahams, J. Candidate preference and hostile humor in the 1968 elections. *Psychol. Rep. 26*, 779-783 (1970).
30. Bippus, A. Factors predicting the perceived effectiveness of politicians' use of humor during a debate. *Humor: International Journal of Humor Research 20*, 105-121 (2007).

Chapter 2
Laugh Codes:
Serious Thoughts about Humorous Comments and the Politicians Who Make Them

Despite growing evidence suggesting that political candidates are often judged almost automatically on the basis of physical attributes such as their facial features,[1-4] height, body size and shape,[5] political events such as debates have long played an important role in shaping public attitudes towards political candidates and willingness to vote for them. Specifically, debates allow the public to place candidates in a side-by-side competitive context and compare them on perceived personal and moral qualities. Not only are candidates more likely to provide information from which the audience may assess psychological attributes such as intelligence and personality and the values they hold,[6-8] but these competitive situations provide a situation where comparative qualities such as status and prestige may be judged.

Although extensive research suggests that presidential debates tend to reinforce candidate and policy preferences of viewers,[9-13] the actions of candidates during the debates may still sway the opinions of undecided voters.[14] Performance by candidates during presidential debates, especially in those situations where the audience's opinion is not fully formed or strongly held, has direct and indirect effects. Specifically, the potential for presidential debates to directly influence public perceptions are accentuated in primary debates. This is because in presidential primary debates there is low information concerning the personal qualities and values of candidates and, as a result, there are no easy decision rules such as party identification to simplify choices.[15] Combined with the presence of multiple candidates to choose from and a public motivated to watch, presidential primary debates have added resonance and salience. This was certainly the case in the 2008 presidential primaries as multiple candidates, ten for the Republican Party and eight for the Democratic Party, jousted with each other over the course of forty debates in the year before the primary elections took place.

The substance of arguments (or lack thereof) put forth by the candidates certainly influences opinions by exposing the candidates as knowledgeable and in touch with party's beliefs, albeit often well after the conclusion of the debate. For instance, President Gerald Ford's mistakenly referring to Poland as not being under Soviet Union dominance during his sole debate with Jimmy Carter in 1976 only became an issue weighing on the minds of voters when it was highlighted by the press. Thus, post-debate press analyses play a powerful role in defining who the winners and losers are by pointing out flaws in knowledge and incongruities in opinions that may have passed unnoticed by the average voter.

In addition, while the public can directly assess the candidates' intelligence and personality and thus their long-term viability as leaders by watching debates, the press plays an important role in determining whether the candidates are perceived as presidential in demeanor and style.[14, 16-18] Here, the ability of candidates to use humor effectively during debates not only attracts audience and media attention, it also gives them the opportunity to define themselves and their target in one brief moment. These defining moments often overshadow the rest of their performance, in other words, allowing the candidates to hit a "home run."

Probably the best example of how one humorous comment can influence an election occurred in the second 1984 presidential debate between incumbent Republican president Ronald Reagan and Democratic Party challenger Walter Mondale. Here, after a disastrous first debate in which Reagan sounded uninformed and confused, a prepared line was given to him in case the age issue was broached. Reagan's resulting comment about not exploiting Mondale's youth and inexperience redirected the criticism in an unexpected direction with the audience laughter, moderator Trewhitt's deferential comment and Mondale's smile signaling respect for the timely witticism. Meanwhile, the resulting shift in attitudes led to a comeback from Reagan, and an evaporation of the age issue despite Reagan likely suffering from early stage Alzheimer's disease.[19, 20] A study later carried out by Fein, Goethals and Kugler[19] suggests that a key element in this game changing moment when Reagan made the quip was the audience laughter that resulted. Without audible laughter, there was no significant change in attitudes towards either candidate as a result of the debate.

Ultimately, whether it is to the voter viewing the debates firsthand, or following the campaign through the mass media, presidential candidates signal their capabilities through humor. The question remains as to whether these signals are honest indicators of intelligence, personality and values or is just so much "cheap talk" distracting from real concerns. The ability for the voter to make the right choice of leader is based upon the ability to discriminate between types of signals, as well as the ability of candidates to honestly signal their capabilities.[21]

In this chapter I attempt to disentangle the complex nature of political humor as it is used on the campaign trail, focusing on presidential primary debates, by first considering the nature of laughter, and the humor that causes it, as social signals. Namely, I consider the evolutionary biology theory of costly signaling and how it influences the relationships between organisms, including predator and prey, potential mating partners, and most pertinently for our analysis, competitors. I next consider the signaling properties of laughter and humor, before turning to the use of humor in political settings and what it signals about both the politician making the humorous comment and the audience laughing at the joke.

Signaling theory and the role of humor

Signaling theory arises from both the fields of economics and evolutionary biology. Within the field of economics, the groundbreaking work of Thorstein Veblen at the turn of the twentieth century introduced the concept of "conspicuous consumption" in which individuals signal their wealth to others through the items they buy.[22] In the words of Veblen, this is "specialized consumption of goods as an evidence of pecuniary strength" (p. 43). This approach to signaling has remained an important part of understanding human and firm behavior for economists and those scholars interested in market interactions[23] although it has only recently incorporated an evolutionary perspective.[24]

Although economic theory provides a more proximate exploration of the influence of cheap talk and costly signals, evolutionary theory, by drawing upon functional premises that work across species, provides theoretical and practical insights that may be applied throughout human interactions. As a result, evolutionary theory's attempt to understand the ultimate causes of behavior is of great value here by providing a unifying framework to work from. Signaling theory here is based upon the premise that many of the adaptations of species occur not just due to the ability to simply survive, but also due to sexual selection, the ability to reproduce at greater rates than competitors. As a result, the complex negotiation of sexual choice and access between males and females is responsible for the development of many personal qualities and their reliable signaling through costly display behavior. As put by Geoffrey Miller[7] "(s)exually selected costly signals typically advertise two classes of traits: good genes or good parenting abilities" (p. 101). Those individuals who choose to mate on the basis of beneficial (or at least neutral) characteristics can be expected to leave more offspring behind with the same characteristics. This in turn influences not only our choice of mating partners, but may also be a factor in how we choose our leaders, especially as there appears to be a relationship between preferred parenting styles, whether liberal or authoritarian, and political ideology.[25]

Two categories of costly signaling consonant with good genes or parenting skills stand out. The first is that of physical fitness in which health, fertility, and youth are signaled through the display of physical attributes as well as through such costly activities such as sports and risk taking behaviors.[6] Indeed, Jared Diamond makes an interesting and compelling argument that such activities as smoking, drinking and recreational drug use are costly signals of physical quality by way of self-handicapping. Specifically, mass consumption of such substances while retaining physical control of oneself suggests individual mastery with the earning of concomitant prestige from peers.[26]

The second major category is that of mental fitness in which intelligence and personality is communicated through problem solving and social skills as well as such costly activities as art, music, poetry and humor.[6] There is obviously an interaction between both physical and mental fitness as physical attributes used in signaling are in and of themselves an indicator of one sort of fitness, while communicating psychological fitness. Specifically, nonverbal displays through the face and through vocalic qualities can not only indicate health, youth and size, but they can also encode humorous messages as well as the successful decoding of these messages through the laughter of its audience. The verbal and concurrent nonverbal displays may also be seen as indicating mental fitness through the cognitive capacity (i.e., intelligence) to both create and recognize incongruity. It also may be seen as demonstrating the psychological characteristics of the participants in the humorous event by displaying the type of humor that the comment maker prefers to make and the appreciation of that humor by the individual laughing.

Here, sense of humor, both in terms of recognizing and producing it, may be seen as an index of personal qualities. Specifically, as intelligence and personality, as well as social values, cannot be effectively signaled through physical properties, it can be "indexed" through performance-based behaviors that are not necessarily as costly to produce but are reliable due to the relative inability for them to be faked.[27] The recognition of humor, as indicated through laughter (and discussed below) is difficult to fake and thus influences others due to its emotion-triggering attributes.[28, 29] The production of humor, as indicated through laughter and discussed below, is quite a bit more complex due to cultural components implicit in its production, and may serve individual and group interests by not only indexing personal qualities, but also serve as, in the words of Thomas Flamson[30] "(A) signaling system that enables group members to covertly assess relative compatibility would therefore present an optimal solution to the within-group assortment problem, and could be favored by selection" (p. 94). In other words, humor serves as an encrypted message that influences those with shared knowledge differentially, allowing for social sorting to occur.[31] Both the laughter that signals humor recognition, and the production of humor that allows for social sorting in a relatively non-coercive and affiliative manner while signaling qualities of the joke-teller play an important, if overlooked, role in politics as we discuss below.

Laughter
Laughter may be seen as a robust and reliable index of sociality for a variety of reasons. Laughter is a hardwired activity with related vocalizations seen across multiple species including rats,[32-33] dogs,[34] and multiple primate species[35] signaling a willingness to engage in playful activities. In humans, spontaneous laughter emerges in 17-26-day-old infants[36] with socially stimulated laughter occurring in infants starting from 3-4 months of age.[37] Furthermore, laughter is seen cross-culturally as well as in deaf and blind children,[38] suggesting an activity innate to humans.

The act of laughter is highly social, occurring thirty times more often in social circumstances in comparison with solitary situations. Even in these solitary situations, laughter may occur due to "pseudo-social" encounters in which a fictional audience is contrived through either imagination or, in the case of television, laugh-tracks.[39] Furthermore, laughter is a highly stereotyped acoustic activity, albeit one that may vary in terms of loudness, length and tone.[40-43] Therefore, while laughter is a highly recognizable vocalization across a range of contexts, its qualities provide physical and social information about the individual(s) laughing through its variation.[44] These qualities may influence perceptions of how affiliative and approachable the signaler(s) might be,[45] likely based upon the influence of the signaler's posture and body tension on their laughter.[43-44]

Thus, laughter may be seen as providing information concerning the connection between the speaker and the audience. Speaker laughter may function to invite his/her audience to laugh[46] or may function to punctuate comments made by the speaker, and communicate playful intent.[47] Furthermore, laughter solidifies bonds by uniting group members through the shared and contagious experience.[48-49] This experience is accentuated by audience size with larger audiences exhibiting greater laughter.[50] This shared experience might also serve to coordinate group response by showing shared consent with and respect for the speaker.[38, 51-53] Even if laughter does not reflect an individual's emotional state, it does serve to signal affiliative intent to unfamiliar persons.[48]

Laughter serves a dual social role. It not only solidifies group unity through the shared and contagious experience of laughter, it can also do so at the expense of others outside of the laughing group. According to Salter (p. 365), "(L)aughter, especially from a group, can be a devastating weapon of intimidation. It signals simultaneously the group's designation of the target as of low status and the mutual affiliation of the group to the exclusion of the target." Here, laughter likely represents symbolic attacks on an individual or group for breaking with the norms of the group doing the laughing [32, 38, 54-56] in a manner that is similar to the "mobbing" of birds and mammals[57] which in the words of Provine is "a synchronized group response by some birds and mammals to drive often larger invaders from their territories" (p.165). Furthermore, if laughter is perceived as coming from members of a shared political party, it was more contagious while the humorous material was rated more positively by respondents than if the same laughter was seen as coming from a political party defined as the out-group.[58] Specifically, humor and the laughter that results allows its practitioners to attack opponents and create socially acceptable hostility belittling their opponents and/or the positions they hold that is then acknowledged and supported by the audience through their laughter.[59, 60]

Humor

Humor, in conjunction with the laughter that results, may not only communicate physical and psychological characteristics, but also communicates characteristics of social situations. Specifically, humor and laughter represent a dialogue between two or more individuals and provide insight into the level of status and prestige both the sender and receiver of a message have, as well as the level of commonality in the information and values they share. Humor also reflects the emotional context of a situation.[39] As a result, humor may be seen as influenced by a complex inter-mixture of physiology, psychology, status and prestige signals and environmental context. At the same time humor can be seen as playing

a robust and accurate role in signaling an individual's intelligence and characteristics of their personality.

John Morreall in his book "Comic relief: A comprehensive philosophy of
humor" sees a basic pattern in humor in which laughter serves as the successful
summation based upon three preconditions: 1) a cognitive shift in which there is
a rapid change of thoughts or perceptions; 2) participants being in a playful
mode; and 3) enjoyment of the cognitive shift.[20] Here, as explored and iterated
by Chafe,[41] the important factor is in "not being earnest." Specifically, whereas
most cognitive shifts are in response to stimuli giving rise to surprise, fear, anger, and confusion, in which case there is little or uncertain amounts of control
and resultant negative emotions, humor, even if it is responding to problems
provides a level of mastery by engaging positive affectivity through a playful
state of mind.[20]

Therefore, humor, by showing mastery of information in a social context
may be seen as a robust indicator of intelligence. Humor can be seen as indexing
intelligence by finding incongruities in normal and less-than-normal social situations. While humor at its best is seen in spur of the moment witticisms as incongruities are noted and commented upon swiftly, humor may also be prepared
ahead of time. In this latter case, the maker of the humorous comment must not
only remember the comment accurately, but also must read the social situation
accurately in order to evince laughter. In both cases, the maker of the comment
signals aptitude with mental processing and the capability to read social situations while performing in a publicly pleasing manner.

Therefore, the use of humor, and to a lesser extent, the ability to recognize
humor, can be seen as a reliable indicator of intelligence. Geoffrey Miller makes
a compelling argument, strongly supported by extensive data, that humor as signaling intelligence is used in sexual selection by both men and women.[6-7, 61] Furthermore, this hard-to-fake signal can be seen as functioning across social domains by indexing interpersonal intelligence and the social dominance that results from effectively wielding it.

Humor is also an effective and sudden way for the person making the humorous comment to leave a lasting and accurate impression, as is the laughter of
those responding to the comment. This shared appreciation for the humor, and
the underlying knowledge and values encrypted within the comment,[31] connects
the parties, indicating potential future cooperative intent. Humor is not only implicated in mating and pair-bonding choice[61, 62] and sustaining successful mar-
riages,[63] the types of humor used are shown to be strongly correlated with the
Big Five personality traits.[61, 64-65] The Big Five in turn has been shown to be
measured reliably, validly predict a range of behaviors, and is stable across life-
span and cultures.[7]

The Big Five model is made up of five personality dimensions that, while
correlated, are independent of each other. These dimensions include: openness
to experience; conscientiousness, which implies prosocial characteristics such as
honesty, integrity, dependability, and reliability; extraversion; individuals high
in agreeableness are more likely to engage in "tend-and-befriend" behaviors and
are more sympathetic and respectful of others; and neuroticism. These dimen-

sions are in turn correlated with both the generation of humor and the specific types of humor preferred by individuals (see Table 2.1). Specifically, Howrigan and MacDonald[64] carried out a study in which they analyzed the relationship between the Big Five and the production of humor, whereas two studies analyzed the relationship between the Big Five and use of humor. For one of these two studies, Martin et al.[65] fashioned a humor styles questionnaire to analyze the relationship between personality characteristics and the use of humor to enhance oneself (self-enhancing), to enhance one's relationship with others (affiliative), to enhance oneself at the expense of others (aggressive), and to enhance relationships at the expense of oneself. The second of these studies, by Greengross and Miller[61] replicated Martin et alia's[65] findings concerning personality and humor style and extended its reach by considering the instrument in light of Geoffrey Miller's application of costly signaling theory to sexual selection.[6/7]

Table 2.1: The relation between the "Big 5" personality traits and humor

	Humor Production	Aggressive Humor	Self-deprecatory Humor	Affiliative Humor
Openness to experience	+			NA/+
Conscientiousness		NA/-	-/-	
Extraversion	+		-/NA	+/+
Agreeableness		-/-	-/-	
Neuroticism			+/+	-/NA

+=significant and positive relationship; -=significant and negative relationship; NA=not significant. Humor production: Howrigan & MacDonald 2008; Humor styles: Greengross & Miller 2008/Martin et al. 2003

Specifically, in consideration of the construction of humor and its relationship to the Big Five personality traits, there appears to be a strong relationship between them, with humor effectively signaling personality. Openness to experience was shown to have a positive relationship with humor generation generally[64] and with affiliative humor style.[65] A negative relationship was seen between the trait of conscientiousness and aggressive humor[65] as well as with self-deprecatory humor.[61, 65] Extraversion was shown to be positively related to humor generation[64] and with the preference for affiliative humor,[61, 65] while showing a negative relationship with self-deprecatory humor.[61] The personality trait agreeableness was negatively related with aggressive and self-deprecatory humor styles,[61, 65] whereas neuroticism was shown to have a positive relationship with self-deprecatory humor style[61, 65] and a negative relationship with affiliative humor style.[61]

Taken together, the ability to produce humor and the preference for different types of humor does tend to do a good job of signaling intelligence and the Big Five personality traits.[6/7] Additionally, humor production, recognition and preference is implicated in sexual selection, both in short- and long-term mates[61/66] as well as the maintenance of these relationships.[63] While there is an accepted positive relationship between dominance and sexual selection, with more powerful individuals obtaining the opportunity to sire and raise more children, the question remains as to whether there is a relationship between dominance and humor, and whether individuals select their leaders with humor in mind.

Therefore, humor may be seen as influencing reproductive outcomes directly and indirectly. It may help potential mates assess each others' intelligence, personality and values more accurately, especially as, in the words of Gervais and Sloan-Wilson,[67] by itself "(L)anguage is a cheap signal that can be used dishonestly and provides no such pleasurable stimulation . . . that is unless conveyed as humor or word play; only then can language elicit in others what is effectively a parallel emotional response" (p. 419). Indirectly, humor may enhance reproductive fitness by allowing more similar individuals to sort themselves into compatible groups to accomplish shared goals in which all members benefit. Furthermore, group members may assert and cement positions of prestige and attendant status within the group through their humor,[21] in turn benefitting their personal rewards and reproductive capacity. In other words, if humor can provide insight into the choice of mating partners based upon it signaling their intelligence, personality and values, humor can likely provide insight into the social and political structures preferred and the politicians chosen by indexing these qualities while divulging encrypted information concerning shared knowledge and values.

Humor in the political process

Humans exhibit a vast array of governing structures ranging from totalitarian structures in which power is vested in one individual to structures that value more equal sharing of power. The presence of political humor becomes most apparent in egalitarian societies, especially when compared to societies where political power is entrenched in one or a limited number of individuals.[68-70] This is due to humans being a socially labile species with individuals exhibiting a strong desire to attain social dominance over others,[71-72] yet giving this chance up to prevent others from having control over them. In more egalitarian societies, humor provides a non-violent means for social control. Specifically, laughter deriving from humorous comments allows for aggression to be communicated without the escalating potential for violence posed by indignation and anger. In the words of Konrad Lorenz[73] "laughter—even at its most intense—is never in danger of regressing and causing the primal aggressive behavior to break through. Barking dogs may occasionally bite, but laughing men hardly ever shoot!" (p. 294).

The target of humorous comments and response to them may be seen as revealing information concerning the nature of the political structures of a society. Specifically, according to Speier,[74] in totalitarian or authoritarian societies humor may only be focused on oneself.[74] Humor at the expense of either those with power or others within the hierarchy in these systems presumes an unacceptable level of individual autonomy and authority. Furthermore, as self-focused humor tends toward the self-deprecatory, the resulting self-imposed loss of prestige may not be worth the effort, especially as power relationship in such situations appear to be "zero-sum" whereas the power, status and prestige gained by one individual often comes at the expense of another.

On the other hand, in societies such as the United States which value equality, political humor often focuses on the political candidates themselves. This may be due to the "non-zero-sum" nature of egalitarian societies where social interactions are fluid and benefit individuals on different metrics. However, humor is rarely focused on the structure and process of the system which allows such sublimated aggression to occur.[75] For instance, political humorists and satirists such as Jon Stewart and Steven Colbert prefer to make fun of the foibles of politicians, often by using the politician's words against them, but rarely if ever make fun of political structures. This stands in contrast to authoritarian political systems, such as the now defunct Soviet Union, where humor at the expense of the political and economic system provided relief from the travails of life, but was only shared amongst trusted associates.[68, 74] As a result, even when a political gadfly such as Congressman Dennis Kucinich makes a humorous comment such as the one he made during the third Democratic Party debate "Now it's interesting the philosophy that's guiding our leaders at every branch of ah, in a executive and judicial branch of government because they go out and tell people 'pull yourselves up by the, by your bootstraps . . . ' and then they steal the boots" that seemingly attacks the political structure of the U.S. government, it is focused on the members of the other two branches of government, although not the system itself.

Table 2.2: Emotional Displays in the Context of Rank

| | | BEHAVIOR & PHYSIOLOGY | |
		Agonistic (competitive)	Affiliative (non-competitive)
RANK	Dominant	**Anger-threat**	**Happiness-reassurance**
	Submissive	**Fear-submission**	**Sadness-appeasement**

From Salter 2007, p. 144.

Power, politics and laughter
Therefore, in societies where strong hierarchical structures conserve political power, and where leaders exert coercion to induce group submission, hedonic activities such as "dominance-play," in which there is inhibition of aggressive behavior signaled through verbal and nonverbal cues (see Table 2.2), are rarely seen. Instead, agonic behavior such as anger and threats by dominant members in turn elicits fear and submission by followers and potential usurpers of their power.[72, 76, 77]

On the other hand, in more egalitarian societies there is an inherent wariness of leaders attempting to gain and exercise power without boundaries. As a result, there may be a series of group social sanctions in response to such leaders attempting to exert their authority beyond acceptable group norms.[71, 78] In such systems, according to Christopher Boehm, those who wish to become leaders must communicate the "absence of arrogance, overbearingness, boastfulness, and personal aloofness" (p. 69) and "espouse a combination of unaggressiveness, generosity, and friendly emotions" (p. 234) prior to taking positions of power. In other words, in egalitarian societies leaders and potential leaders must signal hedonic qualities of affiliation such as happiness-reassurance more than agonic qualities of anger-threat if they want to gain prestige and concomitant followers.[21] As a result, even when aggressive intent is implied, it will likely be mitigated through playful cues such as humor due to egalitarian values inhibiting such lack of politeness.[79] Furthermore, if over-reaching for power is seen to be occurring, humor and ridicule at the expense of the power-seeker may be expected to be forthcoming.

The Dartmouth Group's work analyzing nonverbal social signals[51, 80-82] provides a reliable and valid means of assessing face-to-face dominance interactions between leaders and followers. The framework developed by the Dartmouth group and expanded upon by Salter in turn may be fruitfully applied to the use of humor. Specifically, the different types of humor applied for political ends can be expected to enhance group cohesiveness by inhibiting or punishing behavior that is at variance with group values or may enhance social connections through the positive and rewarding feelings of happiness-reassurance brought about by group laughter. Furthermore, as discussed earlier, the signaling power of laughter has been differentiated into the affiliative display of joyous laughter and the competitive-dominant display of taunting laughter.[45] This in turn may be connected with not only the laughing individual's posture and body tension, in which the face plays a key role,[43, 44] but also in the facial displays of those making humorous comments, as shall be seen in chapter 5.

Power, politics and humor

Humor in egalitarian societies such as the United States may serve as a robust indicator of the personal qualities of the political candidate in terms of his or her intelligence, personality and moral values.[6, 7] This gives citizens critical insight into the individuals they choose their leaders from with information crystallized in what the candidate considers humorous and how effectively they produce it. The information encoded in the humorous comments of a politician may further strengthen the connection with followers if this knowledge is seen as privileged information.[31] It also provides insight into the resilience of leaders and their ability to remain calm and composed in the face of threats to their personal wellbeing. For instance, President Ronald Reagan's quipping 'Honey I forgot to duck' to his wife Nancy after he was shot by a potential assassin did much to reassure a worried nation and cement his legacy.

Humor functions as a leveling mechanism in a political system with egalitarian values, as there is a concomitant distrust of those who would attempt to obtain and abuse political power. Here, humor is used to either bring the speaker closer to the audience through self-deprecatory comments, or the target of humorous comments is placed in an inferior position when compared to the audience (and the speaker) through other-deprecatory comments. In the case of the former, the speaker becomes more accessible and likeable as a result; in the case of the latter, the speaker is able to put the target down while exhibiting cognitive capability and an ability to connect with the audience. An example of this can be seen when Walter Mondale rebutted Gary Hart during the 11 March 1984 Democratic Primary, quipping "When I, when I hear, when I hear your new ideas I'm reminded of that ad 'Where's the beef?'" making reference to a classic Wendy's burger restaurant commercial attacking other burger chains for the lack of substance. This memorable humorous comment mocked Hart's "new ideas" slogan and helped Mondale recapture the primary lead before he ultimately won the Democratic nomination.

Therefore, the two types of humor that can be expected to be seen most often in political campaigns are self-deprecatory and other-deprecatory humor. Both self- and other-deprecatory types of humor tend to serve political ends that are immediate and useful in egalitarian societies, such as making a point or deflecting criticism without direct confrontation. In addition, as discussed earlier, the types of humor used might serve to advertise the intelligence and personality of the candidate. While it is quite likely there is no "pure" example of a candidate solely using one type of humor, the preponderance of one type of humor likely typifies an individual candidate, with humor being a robust indicator of personality.[60, 65] Likewise, preference for one type of humor over another might reflect the preference of supporters, especially as personality attributes measured by the "Big Five" has been tied to political preferences.[83-84]

Self-deprecatory humor

Self-deprecatory humor refers to comments used in an affiliative manner which invites the audience to share in the laughter at their self-targeted foibles. This humor establishes a more equal relationship of identification with the speaker,[85] by highlighting, in a socially pre-emptive manner, the candidate's personal flaws.[61] The use of this sort of humor signals first that the individual sees personal flaws in him or herself and is willing to fully disclose them,[86] but also signals a level of social and general intelligence by being able to elicit laughter.[61] It may also signal the high quality of the person making the comment as individuals making self-deprecatory humorous comments may be seen as engaging in "costly social signaling." Here, the individual making the self-deprecatory comment may be seen as having so much social prestige they can afford to, in essence, give away prestige and make themselves more equal with their audience. An example of this might be seen in the anecdote relayed by Morreall[20] concerning when John F. Kennedy met with schoolchildren at the White House, with one of them asking "Mr. President, how did you become a war hero?" Kennedy answered "It was completely involuntary—they sank my boat" (p. 118). Here, we see that only those individuals with high levels of prestige, and attendant confidence, can afford to make fun of themselves in a public forum, engaging in a form of "conspicuous consumption."

A more recent example, during the 2008 Democratic Party primaries, illustrates the risks and benefits of making self-deprecatory comments when status and prestige are under question. In this case, Governor Bill Richardson, when asked in the New Hampshire Democratic primary debate about mistakes he had made, responded: "I was asked who my favorite Supreme Court justice was. (laughter) And I said (laughter) dead or alive. Um, I should have, I should have stuck to the alive because I then said Whizzer White . . . (laughter) . . . Well then I find out that Whizzer White was against Roe v Wade, against civil rights (laughter). You know, so ah, so that's a, that wasn't, that wasn't a good one (laughter)." Here Richardson, a liberal Latino, made fun of his lack of knowledge by referring to an obvious disconnect between his stated policy preferences and preference for someone who held an opinion opposed to his own. While he was clever with this comment, eliciting audience laughter, this humorous comment may be seen as backfiring in the sense that not only did he point out he made a misstep, but more importantly, he was not in an optimal position to willingly "consume" his status, being a second-tier candidate who had not established his "bona fides" as an intellectually ascendant candidate.

On the other hand, Democratic Party nominee Barack Obama was in a prime position to make fun of himself and his celebrity when, just nineteen days prior to the general election, during the bipartisan Alfred E. Smith dinner he quipped "At least ah we've moved past the days when the main criticism coming from the McCain campaign was that I'm some kind of celebrity. I have to admit that that really hurt. I got so angry about it I punched a paparazzi in the face on my way out of Spago's." Here, Obama had the status and prestige to make such a self-deprecatory comment that was incongruous with his image of being highly self-controlled, yet paid heed to claims concerning his celebrity. John McCain likewise made a series of self- and other-deprecatory comments during this event known for both party's candidates making fun of themselves, their party and their opponent.

Based upon the need for candidates to connect with potential followers by diminishing their status and prestige, it can thus be expected that the great majority of self-referential humor will be self-deprecatory to some degree. Even humor focused on in-group members present at the moment may involve raising the target's status relative to the target. In the first Republican debate, held in Simi Valley, California, several Republican presidential primary candidates, including Mitt Romney, Sam Brownback, Mike Huckabee, and John McCain, weighed in playfully on the possibility of changing the constitution to allow Republican Governor of California Arnold Schwarzenegger to run for president. Of the four, Huckabee and McCain cheekily played the role of pandering politician with Huckabee commenting "(A)fter I've served eight years as President, I'd be happy to change the Constitution for Governor Schwarzenegger," and McCain quipped "Depends on whether he endorses me or not." As a result, the humor used here likely enhanced ties between the speaker and the audience by teasing an audience member as the shared laughter denoted mutual trust.[87]

Other-deprecatory humor
Other-deprecatory, or aggressive, humor differentiates between the speaker and the audience and the target of the humorous comment[85] through disparagement

of someone or something through sarcasm, teasing, ridicule, derision and dispa-ragement.[60, 65] Here laughter plays the role of sublimated aggression, in which there is the signaling of joint hostility towards the intruder on the values of the group.[32, 38, 55, 73] This is an informal type of ostracism in which "moralistic ag-gression" by the group[88] signals concerns about the competing candidate through the mutual assurance of agreement implied by laughter.

A form of this type of humor is ridicule, in which an individual is targeted by focusing on some aspect of that person's behavior, appearance or persona. Ridicule functions by enforcing conformity and enhancing the fear of failure an individual feels. Further, as found by Janes and Olson, this type of humor does not just affect the target, but also the observers of ridicule. Audiences of humor that ridiculed an individual were more likely to be inhibited in their risk taking and were more likely to conform to group behavior expectations.[89] In other words, ridicule functions to enforce group norms by providing an example of ostracism,[88, 90] which in turn functions as a self-policing meta-norm.[55]

During the second Republican Party presidential debate in the 2008 prima-ries, second-tier candidate Tom Tancredo attempted to police his fellow-candidates by ridiculing those changing positions at the same time he evoked religions themes. Here, he commented "You know, it's beginning to, to really sound like a, a Baptist tent revival meeting here, and, and I'm glad to see con-versions, I'm glad they happen, but I must tell you, I trust those conversions when they happen on the road to Damascus and not on the road to Des Moines." Thus, at the same time he played upon two major values, religion and standing by principles, shared by Republican Party members to ridicule opponents, to forge bonds Tancredo also attempted to establish himself as defender of group boundaries. However, while the remark was well crafted, humorous, and used at an appropriate time, the voice perturbations and the awkward delivery evident in the transcribed comments detracted from its impact and Tancredo's attempt to establish himself as a viable candidate.

Individual reception of candidate humor

Attitudes towards both the candidate making the comment and the target of the comment play a role in its reception, especially in the latter stages of a campaign when ties to a candidate have been made and solidified. Specifically, there is a positive relationship between person evaluation and how humorous a comment made by that person is rated. Nabi, Moyer-Gusé and Byrne found participant ratings of humor by comedians Bill Maher and Chris Rock were positively re-lated to source liking and credibility as those participants liking and trusting the comedians found them more humorous.[91] More pertinently for politics, Stewart found that, in an experiment carried out during the latter stages of the 2008 elec-tion, participant attitude towards both John McCain and Barack Obama were strongly related to how positively their humorous comments were evaluated. This evaluation of candidate humorous comments was in turn positively related to how highly participants rated the respective candidates.[92]

Bippus analyzed the influence of self-targeted versus other-targeted humor used by fictional U.S. congressional candidates during the 2004 election cycle finding no significant difference in participant ratings of humor quality between self-directed and opponent-directed humor, a finding replicated by Stewart in his analysis of the 2008 presidential election.[93] However, Bippus found that "(A) candidate's humor was seen as more effective when it was directed at himself as compared to his opponent" (p. 116). This supports a major contention made by many chroniclers of political humor that self-deprecatory humor is perceived as more appropriate, helpful and useful than other-deprecatory humor.[56, 70, 94-96]

Likewise, if a comment disparages the candidate a participant evaluates highly, the judged humorousness of the comment will likely be diminished. This is the case especially with disparaging humor focusing on presidential candidates, as Priest[97] and Abrahams[98] found that ratings of funniness of hostile written jokes about candidates supported by participants were lower than those focused on antagonist candidates.[97-98] However, this effect was only found with McCain supporters when they evaluated humor by Obama disparaging their candidate, John McCain.

In both the case of humorous comments directed toward the in-group or the out-group, the status of the individual performing the humorous comment is enhanced by inducing audience laughter.[60, 99, 100] Specifically, the speaker displays dominance by attaining and maintaining attention[2, 38, 52, 101] and showing cognitive mastery by recognizing incongruities and status by making humorous comments at the expense of others.[102] Indeed, the ability to give nicknames which are often derogatory for the owner, can likewise be seen as asserting social dominance by linking individuals to social positions within a group in a humorous manner.[102] Perhaps most importantly, the speaker is the focal point in distinguishing and enforcing group norms by identifying and encrypting these values in a manner whereas it may be decoded by those individuals sharing pertinent background knowledge, in turn strengthening the bonds between the presumptive leader and potential followers. Thus, individuals using humor effectively can bolster their status and strengthen in-group bonds simultaneously.

Group response to candidate humor

Response to humorous comments can be based not only upon candidate attributes but also by the membership of an individual in a reference group.[49, 103] Ferguson and Ford[59] suggest that this social identity plays a key role in how humorous a comment is considered, with "an individual's self-concept deriving from perceived membership in social groups" (p. 296). This can be seen as the case especially in the context of inter-group competition and the encrypted knowledge that differentiates in-group members from the out-group.

Therefore, it can be expected that political ideology, which is seen as independent of party identification, will play a role in how candidates are evaluated. Party identification has long served as a useful political decision tool[104]; however, recent research suggests emotions play an important role in candidate selection.[105-107] Indeed, personality traits revealing emotional predispositions such as anxiety[25] and disgust[108] might influence political attitudes with conservatives expressing higher levels of these aversive "boundary setting" emotions. At the same time, the type of humor "process" preferred by individuals likely reflects social values concerning certainty, as conservatives are more likely to appreciate humor with resolution compared with liberals, who show greater preference for open-ended/nonsense humor that leaves issues unresolved.[109-111] Therefore, as political humor often deals with moral judgments and functions by resolving the emotional and cognitive incongruities, it can be expected that political ideology will play a role in humor evaluation potentially through the expression of personality attributes.

While self-deprecatory humor may be preferred by Republicans and Democrats alike, Bippus found Republicans, with their strong authoritarian tendencies inclining them to delineate in-group versus out-group,[25] can be seen as more likely to produce other-focused humor. Therefore, humor from Republican candidates ought to focus on the out-group and competitors setting boundaries between themselves and their out-groups, whereas Democratic Party candidates likely will focus their humor on themselves in hopes of being more inclusive, likely reflecting audience humor preferences. This in turn might reflect personality traits esteemed by the parties in a different manner, with Democratic Party identifiers valuing conscientiousness and agreeableness to a greater extent than their Republican Party counterparts.

Conclusion

In political debates the targets of humorous comments ought to range from the out-group, with humor disparaging individual competitors or rival groups, to the in-group, with playful, non-offensive humor being used, and finally to non-aligned individuals, with speakers likely using either playful or, at the least, non-alienating humor. The targets of humorous comments focused on the out-group are those individuals and organizations considered consensus enemies of the audience. Direct competitors to the speaker may be considered a part of the out-group with the speaker attempting to drive the audience away from rival candidates. At the same time, the speaker can expect to acquire supporters by establishing the behavioral boundaries of group expectations.[89] As political humor tends to disparage the opposition more often than not, it is expected that individual competitors and out-groups will bear the brunt of humorous comments. However, it should be noted that while competitors will invariably be targets, their future viability as allies may mitigate the extent of damage intended by the speaker.

Another key attribute of humorous comments, and the laughter that results, is the social sorting that occurs when encrypted knowledge is shared, leading the forging of stronger connecting between the candidate and in-group followers. Here, the in-group may be defined as an inclusive group, but also one that may be subdivided further to include supporters not present and those that are present in the audience. In addition, non-aligned individuals, such as moderators, may become the target of humorous comments by virtue of interacting with the contending candidates, although the nature of these comments might be more that of politeness allowing for conflict to be skirted. In other words, it is expected humor will be more affiliative and bring people together. Finally, the speaker him/herself, as well as his/her family, may be the focus of humorous comments.

However, it is fully expected these jibes will be more affiliative-focused and non-threatening.

The question concerning the impact humorous comments have in the larger political arena remains to be explored. In other words, how well do humorous comments and the audience laughter that results translate into media coverage and financial support for presidential candidates? I focus on this in the next chapter.

References

1. Little, A. C., Burriss, R. P., Jones, B. C. & Roberts, S. C. Facial appearance affects voting decisions. *Evolution and Human Behavior* 28, 18-27 (2007).
2. Mazur, A. in *Biosociology of dominance and deference* (Rowman & Little-field, Lanham, MD, 2005).
3. Poutvaara, P., Jordahl, H. & Berggren, N. Faces of politicians: Babyfacedness predicts inferred competence but not electoral success. *J. Exp. Soc. Psychol.* 45, 1132-1135 (2009).
4. Todorov, A., Mandisodza, A. N., Goren, A. & Hall, C. C. Inferences of competence from faces predict election outcomes. *Science* 308, 1623 (2005).
5. Sell, A. *et al.* Human adaptations for the visual assessment of strength and fighting ability from the body and face. *Proceedings of the Royal Society B: Biological Sciences* 276, 575-584 (2009).
6. Miller, G. F. in *The mating mind: How sexual choice shaped the evolution of human nature* (Doubleday Books, New York, NY, 2000).
7. Miller, G. F. Sexual selection for moral virtues. *Q. Rev. Biol.* 82, 97-125 (2007).
8. Miller, G. in *Spent: sex, evolution, and consumer behavior* (Viking, New York, 2009).
9. Benoit, W. L. & Hansen, G. J. Presidential Debate Watching, Issue Knowledge, Character Evaluation, and Vote Choice. *Human Communication Research* 30, 121-144 (2004).
10. Benoit, W. L., McKinney, M. S. & Stephenson, M. T. Effects of Watching Primary Debates in the 2000 U.S. Presidential Campaign. *J. Commun.* 52, 316 (2002).
11. Lang, G. E. & Lang, K. Immediate and Delayed Responses to a Carter-Ford Debate: Assessing Public Opinion. *The Public Opinion Quarterly* 42, 322-341 (1978).
12. Yawn, M., Ellsworth, K., Beatty, B. & Kahn, K. F. How a presidential primary debate changed attitudes of audience members. *Polit. Behav.* 20, 155-181 (1998).
13. Ziegler, R., Arnold, F. & Diehl, M. Communication modality and biased processing: A study on the occasion of the German 2002 election TV debate. *Basic and applied social psychology* 29, 175-184 (2007).
14. Racine Group. White paper on televised political campaign debates. *Argumentation and Advocacy* 38, 199-218 (2002).

15. Lanoue, D. J. & Schrott, P. R. in *The Joint Press Conference: The history, impact, and prospects of American presidential debates* 173 (Greenwood Press, Westport, CT, 1991).
16. Benoit, W. L., Stein, K. A. & Hansen, G. J. Newspaper Coverage of Presidential Debates. *Argumentation & Advocacy* 41, 17-27 (2004).
17. Jamieson, K. H. & Waldman, P. in *The press effect: politicians, journalists, and the stories that shape the political world* 220 (Oxford University Press, Oxford; New York, 2004).
18. Newton, J. S., Masters, R. D., McHugo, G. J. & Sullivan, D. G. Making up our minds: Effects of network coverage on viewer impressions of leaders. *Polity* 20, 226-246 (1987).
19. Fein, S., Goethals, G. R. & Kugler, M. B. Social Influence on Political Judgments: The Case of Presidential Debates. *Polit. Psychol.* 28, 165-192 (2007).
20. Morreall, J. in *Comic relief: A comprehensive philosophy of humor* 187 (Wiley-Blackwell, Malden, MA, 2009).
21. Henrich, J. & Gil-White, F. J. The evolution of prestige: Freely conferred deference as a mechanism for enhancing the benefits of cultural transmission. *Evolution and Human Behavior* 22, 165-196 (2001).
22. Veblen, T. in *The theory of the leisure class* (Oxford University Press, USA, New York, NY, 2007).
23. Spence, M. Signaling in retrospect and the informational structure of markets. *Am. Econ. Rev.* 92, 434-459 (2002).
24. Saad, G. in *The evolutionary bases of consumption* 339 (Lawrence Erlbaum, Mahwah, NJ, 2007).
25. Hetherington, M. J. & Weiler, J. D. in *Authoritarianism and polarization in American politics* 234 (Cambridge University Press, New York, 2009).
26. Diamond, J. M. in *The third chimpanzee: The evolution and future of the human animal* 424 (Harper Collins, New York, NY, 1992).
27. Maynard-Smith, J. & Harper, D. in *Animal signals* (Oxford Univ. Press, New York, NY, 2003).
28. Owren, M. J., Rendall, D. & Ryan, M. J. Redefining animal signaling: influence versus information in communication. *Biology and Philosophy*, 1-26 (2010).
29. Rendall, D., Owren, M. J. & Ryan, M. J. What do animal signals mean? *Anim. Behav.* 78, 233-240 (2009).
30. Flamson, T. The encryption theory: Studies in Brazil and the United States testing an evolutionary explanation of humor as an honest signal. University of California, Las Angeles, 1-167 (2010).
31. Flamson, T. & Barrett, H. C. The encryption theory of humor: A knowledge-based mechanism of honest signaling. *Journal of Evolutionary Psychology* 6, 261-281 (2008).
32. Panksepp, J. in *Affective neuroscience: the foundations of human and animal emotions* 466-466 (Oxford University Press, New York, 1998).

33. Panksepp, J. Neuroevolutionary sources of laughter and social joy: Modeling primal human laughter in laboratory rats. *Behav. Brain Res.* 182, 231-244 (2007).
34. Faragó, T., Pongrácz, P., Range, F., Virányi, Z. & Miklósi, Á. 'The bone is mine': affective and referential aspects of dog growls. *Anim. Behav.* 79, 917-925 (2010).
35. Preuschoft, S. & Van Hooff, J. The social function of "smile" and "laughter": Variations across primate species and societies. *Nonverbal communication: Where nature meets culture*, 171–190 (1997).
36. Kawakami, K. *et al.* Spontaneous smile and spontaneous laugh: An intensive longitudinal case study. *Infant Behavior and Development* 30, 146-152 (2007).
37. Provine, R. R. in *Laughter: A scientific investigation* (Penguin Press, New York, NY, 2001).
38. Eibl-Eibesfeldt, I. in *Human ethology* 848 (Aldine De Gruyter, New York, 1989).
39. Fridlund, A. J. in *Human facial expression: An evolutionary view* (Academic Press, San Diego, CA, 1994).
40. Bachorowski, J. & Owren, M. J. Not All Laughs Are Alike: Voiced but Not Unvoiced Laughter Readily Elicits Positive Affect. *Psychological Science* 12, 252-257 (2001).
41. Chafe, W. in *The importance of not being earnest: the feeling behind laughter and humor* (John Benjamins Publishing Co, 2007).
42. Grammer, K. & Eibl-Eibesfeldt, I. The ritualisation of laughter. *Natürlichkeit der Sprache und der Kultur*, 192-214 (1990).
43. Ruch, W. & Ekman, P. The expressive pattern of laughter. *Emotion, qualia, and consciousness*, 426-443 (2001).
44. Zahavi, A. & Zahavi, A. in *The handicap principle: A missing piece of Darwin's puzzle* 286 (Oxford University Press, New York, NY, 1997).
45. Szameitat, D. P. *et al.* Differentiation of emotions in laughter at the behavioral level. *Emotion* 9, 397-405 (2009).
46. Jefferson, G. A technique for inviting laughter and its subsequent acceptance/declination. *Everyday language: Studies in ethnomethodology* 79, 79-96 (1979).
47. Provine, R. R. Laughter punctuates speech: Linguistic, social and gender contexts of laughter. *Ethology* 95, 291-298 (1993).
48. Devereux, P. G. & Ginsburg, G. P. Sociality effects on the production of laughter. *J. Gen. Psychol.* 128, 227-240 (2001).
49. Hatfield, E., Cacioppo, J. T. & Rapson, R. L. Emotional contagion. *Current Directions in Psychological Science*, 96-99 (1993).
50. Provine, R. R. Contagious laughter: Laughter is a sufficient stimulus for laughs and smiles. *Bulletin of the Psychonomic Society* 30, 1-4 (1992).
51. Masters, R. D. in *The nature of politics* 298-298 (Yale University Press, New Haven, 1989).
52. Salter, F. K. in *Emotions in command: Biology, bureaucracy, and cultural evolution* (Transaction Pub, New Brunswick, NJ, 2007).

53. Stillman, T. F., Baumeister, R. F. & DeWall, C. N. What's So Funny About Not Having Money? The Effects of Power on Laughter. *Person. Soc. Psychol Bull.* 33, 1547-1558 (2007).

54. Alexander, R. Ostracism and Indirect Reciprocity: The Reproductive Significance of Humor. *Ethology and Sociobiology 7* (1986).

55. Axelrod, R. M. in *The complexity of cooperation: Agent-based models of competition and collaboration* (Princeton University Press, Princeton, NJ, 1997).

56. Yarwood, D. L. in *When Congress makes a joke: Congressional humor then and now* 161 (Rowman & Littlefield Publishers, Inc., Lanham, MD, 2004).

57. Provine, R. R. in *The psychology of facial expression.*(ed. Fernández-Dols, J. M.) 158-175 (Cambridge University Press; Editions de la Maison des Sciences de l'Homme, New York, NY; Paris, France, 1997).

58. Platow, M. J. *et al.* "It's not funny if they're laughing": Self-categorization, social influence, and responses to canned laughter. *J. Exp. Soc. Psychol.* 41, 542-550 (2005).

59. Ford, T. E. & Ferguson, M. A. Social Consequences of Disparagement Humor: A Prejudiced Norm Theory. *Personality & Social Psychology Review.* 8, 79-94 (2004).

60. Martin, R. A. in *The psychology of humor: An integrative approach* (Elsevier, Amsterdam, Netherlands, 2007).

61. Greengross, G. & Miller, G. F. Dissing oneself versus dissing rivals: Effects of status, personality, and sex on the short-term and long-term attractiveness of self-deprecating and other-deprecating humor. *Evolutionary Psychology* 6, 393-408 (2008).

62. Bressler, E. R. & Balshine, S. The influence of humor on desirability. *Evolution and Human Behavior* 27, 29-39 (2006).

63. Campbell, L., Martin, R. A. & Ward, J. R. An observational study of humor use while resolving conflict in dating couples. *Personal Relationships* 15, 41-55 (2008).

64. Howrigan, D. P. & MacDonald, K. B. Humor as a mental fitness indicator. *Evolutionary Psychology* 6, 625–666 (2008).

65. Martin, R. A., Puhlik-Doris, P., Larsen, G., Gray, J. & Weir, K. Individual differences in uses of humor and their relation to psychological well-being: Development of the Humor Styles Questionnaire. *Journal of Research in Personality* 37, 48-75 (2003).

66. Bressler, E. R., Martin, R. A. & Balshine, S. Production and appreciation of humor as sexually selected traits. *Evolution and Human Behavior* 27, 121-130 (2006).

67. Gervais, M. & Wilson, D. S. The evolution and functions of laughter and humor: a synthetic approach. *Q. Rev. Biol.* 80, 395-430 (2005).

68. Dmitriev, A. V. Humor and Politics. *Anthropology & Archeology of Eurasia* 44, 64-100 (2006).

69. Paletz, D. L. Political humor and authority: From support to subversion. *International Political Science Review/Revue internationale de science politique* 11, 483-493 (1990).

70. Udall, M. K. in *Too funny to be President* 249 (The University of Arizona Press, Tucson, AZ, 1988).
71. Boehm, C. in *Hierarchy in the forest: the evolution of egalitarian behavior* 292-292 (Harvard University Press, Cambridge, MA, 1999).
72. Somit, A. & Peterson, S. A. in *Darwinism, dominance, and democracy: The biological bases of authoritarianism* 141 (Praeger, Westport, CT, 1997).
73. Lorenz, K. in *On aggression* (Psychology Press, New York, NY, 2002).
74. Speier, H. Wit and politics: An essay on laughter and power. *American journal of sociology*, 1352-1401 (1998).
75. Boskin, J. American political humor: Touchables and taboos. *International Political Science Review* 11, 473-482 (1990).
76. Masters, R. D. & Sullivan, D. G. Nonverbal displays and political leadership in France and the United States. *Polit. Behav.* 11, 123-156 (1989).
77. Tiedens, L. Z. & Fragale, A. R. Power moves: Complementarity in dominant and submissive nonverbal behavior. *J. Pers. Soc. Psychol.* 84, 558 (2003).
78. Smith, K. B., Larimer, C. W., Littvay, L. & Hibbing, J. R. Evolutionary theory and political leadership: Why certain people do not trust decision makers. *The Journal of Politics* 69, 285-299 (2007).
79. Dailey, W. O., Hinck, E. A. & Hinck, S. S. Audience Perceptions of Politeness and Advocacy Skills in the 2000 and 2004 Presidential Debates. *Argumentation and Advocacy* 41, 196-210 (2005).
80. Sullivan, D. G. & Masters, R. D. 'Happy Warriors': Leaders' Facial Displays, Viewers' Emotions, and Political Support. *Am. J. Polit. Sci.* 32, 345-368 (1988).
81. Masters, R. D., Sullivan, D. G., Lanzetta, J. T., McHugo, G. J. & Englis, B. G. The facial displays of leaders: Toward an ethology of human politics. *J. Soc. Biol. Struct.* 9, 319-343 (1986).
82. Stewart, P. A., Salter, F. K. & Mehu, M. Taking leaders at face value: Ethology and the analysis of televised leader displays. *Politics and the Life Sciences* 28, 48-74 (2009).
83. Gerber, A. S., Huber, G. A., Doherty, D., Dowling, C. M. & Ha, S. E. Personality and political attitudes: Relationships across issue domains and political contexts. *American Political Science Review* 104, 111-133 (2010).
84. Hirsh, J. B. & DeYoung, C. G. Compassionate liberals and polite conservatives: Associations of agreeableness with political ideology and moral values. *Person. Soc. Psychol Bull.* 36, 655 (2010).
85. Meyer, J. C. Humor as a Double-Edged Sword: Four Functions of Humor in Communication. *Communication Theory* 10, 310-331 (2000).
86. Frank, R. H. in *Passions within reason: The strategic role of the emotions.* (WW Norton & Co, New York, NY, 1988).
87. Mehu, M. & Dunbar, R. I. M. Relationship between smiling and laughter in humans (homo sapiens): Testing the power asymmetry hypothesis. *Folia Primatol.* 79, 269-280 (2008).
88. Masters, R. D. Ostracism as a social and biological phenomenon: An introduction. *Ethol. Sociobiol.* 7, 149-158 (1986).

89. Janes, L. M. & Olson, J. M. Jeer pressures: The behavioral effects of observing ridicule of others. *Person. Soc. Psychol Bull.* 26, 474-485 (2000).
90. Weisfeld, G. E. The adaptive value of humor and laughter. *Ethology & Sociobiology* 14, 141-169 (1993).
91. Nabi, R. L., Moyer-Guseé, E. & Byrne, S. All Joking Aside: A Serious Investigation into the Persuasive Effect of Funny Social Issue Messages. *Communication Monographs* 74, 29-54 (2007).
92. Stewart, P. A. The influence of self- and other-deprecatory humor on presidential candidate evaluation during the 2008 election. *Social Science Information* 50, 201-222 (2011).
93. Bippus, A. Factors predicting the perceived effectiveness of politicians' use of humor during a debate. *Humor: International Journal of Humor Research* 20, 105-121 (2007).
94. Gardner, G., & Gardner, G. Mocking of the president, in *Campaign comedy: political humor from Clinton to Kennedy* (Wayne State University Press, Detroit, 1994).
95. Schutz, C. E. in *Political humor: from Aristophanes to Sam Ervin* (Fairleigh Dickinson University Press, Rutherford NJ, 1977).
96. Sloane, A. A. in *Humor in the White House: the wit of five American presidents* 208 (McFarland & Co Inc Pub, Jefferson, NC, 2001).
97. Priest, R. F. Election jokes: The effects of reference group membership. *Psychol. Rep.* 18, 600-602 (1966).
98. Priest, R. F. & Abrahams, J. Candidate preference and hostile humor in the 1968 elections. *Psychol. Rep.* 26, 779-783 (1970).
99. Keltner, D., Young, R. C., Heerey, E. A., Oemig, C. & Monarch, N. D. Teasing in hierarchical and intimate relations. *J. Pers. Soc. Psychol.* 75, 1231-1247 (1998).
100. Keltner, D., Capps, L., Kring, A. M., Young, R. C. & Heerey, E. A. Just teasing: A conceptual analysis and empirical review. *Psychol. Bull.* 127, 229-248 (2001).
101. Chance, M. R. A. Attention Structure as the Basis of Primate Rank Orders. *Man* 2, 503-518 (1967).
102. Fine, G. A. & de Soucey, M. Joking cultures: Humor themes as social regulation in group life. *Humor: International Journal of Humor Research* 18, 1-22 (2005).
103. Smith, E. R., Seger, C. R. & Mackie, D. M. Can emotions be truly group level? Evidence regarding four conceptual criteria. *J. Pers. Soc. Psychol.* 93, 431 (2007).
104. Campbell, A., Converse, P. E., Miller, W. E. & Stokes, D. E. in *The American voter* 573 (Wiley, New York, 1960).
105. Brader, T. in *Campaigning for hearts and minds: How emotional appeals in political ads work* (University Of Chicago Press, Chicago, IL, 2006).
106. Marcus, G. E., Neuman, W. R. & MacKuen, M. in *Affective intelligence and political judgment* (University of Chicago Press, Chicago, IL, 2000).
107. Neuman, W. R., Marcus, G. E., Crigler, A. N. & Mackuen, M. in *The affect effect* (University of Chicago Press, Chicago, IL. 2007).

108. Inbar, Y., Pizarro, D. A. & Bloom, P. Conservatives are more easily dis-
    gusted than liberals. *Cognition & Emotion* 23, 714-725 (2009).
109. Hehl, F. & Ruch, W. Conservatism as a predictor of responses to humour–
    IIII. The prediction of appreciation of incongruity-resolution based humour
    by content saturated attitude scales in five samples* 1. *Personality and in-
    dividual differences* 11, 439-445 (1990).
110. Ruch, W. & Hehl, F. Conservatism as a predictor of responses to humour–
    II. The location of sense of humour in a comprehensive attitude space* 1.
    Personality and Individual Differences 7, 861-874 (1986).
111. Ruch, W. & Hehl, F. Conservatism as a predictor of responses to humour–
    I: A comparison of four scales. *Personality and individual differences* 7, 1-
    14 (1986).

Chapter 3
Laughing All the Way to the Bank:
Audience Laughter, Media, and Money

The influence of debates on electoral outcomes is rarely disputed. As a result, Presidential debates have been systematically studied by political scientists since at least the 1960 Kennedy-Nixon encounter, as this first nationally broadcast debate captivated the nation, attracting the most television viewers to date.[12] Although research has been carried out over the past half century, questions still remain concerning how extensively debates can affect voting behavior. Of particular interest are the mechanisms by which debates affect public attitudes towards the candidates, especially with early season debates where candidates attempt to define themselves in front of the press and the public.

Campaign events such as debates affect electoral outcomes both directly and indirectly. Debates have a direct effect by swaying public opinion through candidate performance. Studies find that although debates tend to reinforce previously held candidate and policy preferences,[3-7] in some cases debates may still directly sway the opinions of undecided voters, with the candidates' appearance as presidential in demeanor and style playing an important role.[1, 6] This ability to directly affect voters' opinions and win their support is attenuated early in the campaign season where even educated partisans may have little or no information about specific candidates.

A major indicator of candidate support comes in terms of financial contributions from would-be followers. Specifically, individuals "put their money where their mouth is" by donating to favored candidates, especially in the early primary season. The ability to give money directly to presidential candidates during the primaries has been enhanced by changes to campaign finance regulations[8] as well as by the ability for supporters to give money directly through the Internet. Therefore, support for presidential candidates may be seen both in the number of contributions made and the amount given.

Indirectly, debates affect attitudes through media attention to the candidate, which in turn affects the public's attitudes toward the candidates.[9-11] Post-debate press analyses define who the winners and losers are, as well as providing information about the character of the candidates and their viability as leaders.[1, 6, 12-14] The resultant media coverage further influences the public's perceptions of the candidates through the quality and quantity of coverage given. As a result, candidates wishing to establish themselves as *the* leading contender will attempt to utilize not only pre-debate pitch and post-debate spin, in which expectations and interpretation of performance are posited by campaign operatives,[15] but most obviously will want to put in a memorable performance.

Therefore, presidential primary debates in particular are especially salient by setting the tone early in the presidential campaign cycle. By putting multiple candidates in a side-by-side setting, performance determines media coverage and, ultimately, viability. Comparisons by citizens and the media may be made to determine the best candidate for each political party's contender for president of the United States. While the ability to demonstrate policy knowledge and present solutions to political problems certainly plays a role, other attributes are important for separating out the viable "front-running" candidates from the "long-shots." Specifically, being able to attain and maintain attention during the primary debates plays a key role in signaling to both citizens viewing the debates, and the media covering them, the value of candidates as presidential timber. Likewise, being able to elicit emotional response, such as laughter, from the audience in attendance signals to both the viewers at home and media outlets covering the event the extent of connection made between potential supporters and putative leaders. In other words, debate performance ought to be able to affect media coverage and extent of political support.

This chapter addresses three research questions concerning presidential primary debates that occur early in the electoral season, well before the primaries and caucuses that determine the presidential candidates for each party. First, I ascertain whether early debates make a difference in attention given to presidential candidates. Specifically, while in the words of David Damore[16] "disproportionate levels of media coverage are given to early contests to overcome uncertainty about the campaign and candidates" (p. 351), the question remains as to whether the early debates will attract media attention for the participating candidates, in turn increasing the amount of public recognition and financial support they receive. Second, I consider whether candidates are defined as either front-runner or long-shot early in the electoral season by the mass media and by individual contributors, well in advance of the voters having made their voices heard. Third, this chapter will consider whether debate performance itself influences media coverage and individual financial support. Here both dominance of attention and the use of humor by presidential candidates to obtain media attention are considered. Dominance of attention is defined as proportion of time a candidate is allotted to speak, although it may be influenced by the status of the candidate prior to the debates. On the other hand, humor, signaled by the elicitation of audience laughter and the strength of that laughter, reflects a contemporaneous connection with the audience and may be seen as reflecting candidate performance qualities, and may be the one aspect of debate performance not affected by prior status.

Media coverage and charisma—Humorous comments at work

Although extensive research concerning presidential debates during the general election season has been carried out (see The Racine Group 2002 for an excellent synopsis), relatively few scholars do research concerning primary debates.[4,] [17, 18] This is especially the case with debates taking place at the very outset of presidential campaigns when candidates attempt to define themselves as viable. Primary debates present differences from general election debates, both thematically and structurally. The first and most obvious difference between primary and general election debates is the partisan nature of primary debates. Here the emphasis tends not to be so much in-kind policy differences but differences in degree as the candidates position themselves to obtain the support of strong partisans most likely to vote in the primaries.[18] Therefore, while competition does indeed remain the focus of such events, it is collegial and differences tend to be attenuated.

The first question that needs to be addressed is whether primary debates, especially those early in the electoral season, affect the media coverage and individual electoral support of presidential candidates. Presumably, significant attention will be given to these early debates by the print media and radio and television outlets wishing to divine the viability of candidates in the crowded primary field and individual contributors who wish to support those candidates exhibiting leadership qualities. Specifically, media mentions of candidates can be expected to increase as a result of participation in debates as will tangible political support in the form of the number and amount of individual FEC contributions.

Second, by having more candidates than is the norm in general election debates, even in the case of late primary debates where the "pretenders" have removed themselves from contention, the form and, hence, the outcome of the debates are altered. As pointed out by The Racine Group[1] "Multiple candidate debates reduce the amount of time each candidate has to respond, the number of topics covered, depth of analysis, opportunities for defense as well as attack, and the direction of candidates' address. Primary debate formats often provide no opportunity for candidates answering at the beginning of a sequence to respond to the candidates who follow" (p. 205). In essence, candidates in primary debates are constrained in the way they showcase their leadership abilities by being unable to respond to policy particulars. Instead, the focus is, indeed must be, on stylistic performance. As pointed out by Lanoue and Schrott,[17] "In short, when issue positions are largely indistinguishable, perhaps image and style are the only reasonable bases on which to evaluate the candidates" (p. 301).

Although proportion of time given to candidates might be relatively constrained, treatment given to candidates may differ based upon their status as front-runners or long-shots. A variety of factors may be responsible for a candidate's position as a serious candidate for the presidency, as is seen with the 2008 presidential primaries. The candidate may have previously been a serious contender, as was the case with John Edwards and John McCain, who were serious challengers for their respective party's nomination in previous elections, or may have had other national-level leadership credentials, as was the case with Hillary

Clinton, wife of ex-President Bill Clinton and high profile New York Senator, and Rudy Giuliani, New York City mayor with emotional linkage with September 11, 2001 and its aftermath. Likewise, the candidate might currently occupy or have recently occupied a high profile position which keeps them in the public eye, as is the case with late addition to the Republican race, ex-Senator and television actor Fred Thompson.

Ultimately, the major indicator of a candidate's status as a serious candidate is the attention he or she obtains from the mass media.[9] This dominance of attention is well established as an indicator of status not only with humans, but with animal species in which there is a hierarchical social structure.[19-21] Therefore, while normally seen in face-to-face encounters, dominance can be and has been extrapolated to the virtual face-to-face interaction of television and the new media[22] and plays a major role in asserting the viability of political candidates as leaders.[23, 24] In order to be chosen as a leader, one must look and act like a viable leader which is in turn preconditioned on having potential followers paying attention.[25, 26] In this case, it is the media paying attention and cueing the public as to which candidate is worthy of further attention. Therefore, it can be expected that the high profile candidates for both parties will have greater media coverage, both prior to the debates and during the debates and political support from individuals in terms of number and amount of financial contributions.

A major factor behind dominance of attention, and one that is not as well specified, may be seen as falling under the umbrella concept of charisma. A candidate possessing charisma has the definitive, albeit not well defined, advantage in drawing the attention of the media by virtue of already possessing this emergent quality indicative of an affective connection between followers and a leader. Research to date has underscored the importance of emotional response to candidates for their political success. Specifically, candidates able to elicit positive emotional response are more likely to win elections.[27, 28]

More "charismatic" leaders are able to build affiliation within a group through reassurance gestures or enhance group stability through the display of their dominance.[20, 21, 29] In short, the ability of leaders to elicit appropriate emotional responses enhances their ability to affect social behavior. While the ability to engender fear in potential opponents[30, 31] and respond to external threats by rallying followers to a cause[28, 32-34] are key components of leadership, the ability to use affiliative behavior to elicit positive emotional response and freely conferred deference is the major tool available to candidates.[35]

This is especially the case in debates when the candidates are in a side-by-side comparative setting.[36] Here viewers can monitor their emotional response and cognitive evaluations, whether positive or negative, to each candidate. Regardless of whether their response is conscious or preconscious,[34, 37] these evaluations will likely affect both citizen perceptions and media coverage.[23]

Along with smiling, a social behavior done mainly in the presence of others to indicate mutual support, laughter likewise promotes affiliation of individuals with each other. Due to its contagious nature, individual and group ties are consolidated and cemented by laughter.[22] Laughter may also serve to show respect to the speaker, as commented upon by Irenäus Eibl-Eibesfeldt "(R)espect is shown in self-deprecation, often regressing into infantilisms, giggling, laughing and appearing to be helpless" (p. 508). This respect may be based upon an appreciation for the speaker's cleverness in identifying incongruities, whether in him or herself or in competitors, as well as the speaker's mastery of a challenging situation.[38] Regardless of the target, audience laughter signifies a bond between the audience and the source of the humorous utterance, an emotional connection indicating charismatic leadership qualities and/or similarities between the speaker and the audience.

It is expected that having a sense of humor will affect reception of candidates, regardless of whether they are a front-runner or second tier candidate. Specifically, by inducing a sense of social solidarity through the emotional contagion of laughter, candidates will likely garner more media attention. Furthermore, the stronger the audience response in terms of laughter, the more likely that candidate will reap the benefits of being a humorous individual. As a result, it can be expected that the more humorous comments made by candidates, the more media coverage they will receive and the more financial support they will receive from individuals in the public. In addition, it is expected that the stronger the audience response to humorous comments by candidates in terms of judged laughter strength, they will likewise receive more media coverage and financial support.[a]

The 2008 presidential primaries

This chapter ascertains changes in media coverage of presidential candidates as a result of their performance during the initial primary debates during the 2008 presidential primary season. It does so by looking at a total of six presidential primary debates, with the initial three for each political party providing cases. As I am interested in the influence of candidate performance during the debate on media coverage and financial support from individuals, we treat these events as independent by pooling candidate performance in each debate, providing a total of fifty-four cases for analysis. [b]

I specifically consider change in mentions of each presidential primary candidate in the mass media and change in levels of individual financial support from the period five days prior to the debate to five days after the debate. Change in mass media coverage considers how many mentions are made of each candidate's name in the print media and on radio and television outlets in the five days prior to and five days after the primary debate under consideration. The data concerning mass media print coverage was retrieved from the Lexis-Nexis Major News Outlet function and came from sources such as the New York Times, New York Daily News, Boston Globe, Washington Post, Wall Street Journal, and other high impact newspapers. Likewise, mass media coverage through radio and television was constructed by using the LexisNexis search function for all transcripts on line. The search function was utilized for each candidate for each of the debates considered. Thus, it is possible to observe and analyze the impact of candidate debate performance on media attention for the major news publications.

Although number of mentions of the presidential candidate's name may be considered an incomplete and even an inferior measure when compared to studies considering favorability of news coverage to presidential candidates[10-12] or visual frames of the candidates themselves,[23] it provides a useful proxy for analysis. Specifically, presidential primaries may be seen as more about recognition than frames with candidates attempting to gain name recognition from the public.[9, 18] Therefore, especially in the early primary season, candidate name mentions can be considered an appropriate measure of media coverage and, concomitantly, the public attention that results. Furthermore, these newspapers the data were sourced from provide the hub of news sources for Internet blogging.[39]

Perhaps the most valid and reliable measure of campaign interest is that of individual campaign contributions.[8, 16] As is the case for media coverage, contribution data is collected for the five days prior to the debate and the five days after the debate, with the Federal Elections Commission (FEC) online databases for each presidential candidate providing the basis for the variable created here. The data extracted provides information concerning how many individuals gave money to each of the candidates and how much total money was given.

Table 3.1a: Republican Party Presidential Candidate Debate Performance

	Proportion speaking time	Humorous comments	Mean Laughter Scale	Change in print media coverage	Change in radio-TV coverage	Change in FEC contributions	Change in FEC contributors
Brownback	.103	.333	.667	14.667	67.000	16340.93	10.00
Gilmore	.093	.333	.333	7.667	28.000	-10033.33	-6.67
Giuliani	.123	2.000	1.944	24.000	402.667	-211925.00	-259.33
Huckabee	.081	2.667	3.333	19.000	201.333	47852.60	48.67
Hunter	.075	1.333	1.833	13.667	39.667	-5720.00	-4.33
McCain	.139	3.000	3.250	28.000	561.333	-66007.53	-32.00
Paul	.088	.667	1.167	23.333	316.333	59735.68	119.00
Romney	.143	1.333	1.167	13.667	281.000	4452.36	107.33
Tancredo	.086	.667	1.167	21.000	115.333	-1894.33	31.00
T. Thompson	.070	1.000	.444	10.333	155.333	-5991.40	-6.00

Variables considering debate performance look at the proportion of time each candidate was given to speak during the debate, the number of humorous comments made by each candidate during the respective debates, and the strength of the laughter, on average, during each debate. First, in creating the variable concerning proportion of speaking time, each debate was coded for how much speaking time in seconds each candidate was given. Only those utterances of greater than three seconds in length were considered, excluding short interruptions to instead identify concerted attention on the candidate making tangible utterances. The total speaking time each candidate received during the debate under consideration was summed with the other contenders then divided by the individual time speaking to provide the proportion of speaking time. This provides insight into the amount of attention each candidate was given during the debates, providing an indicator of the status and prestige they were accorded by the moderators.

Table 3.1b: Democratic Party Presidential Candidate Debate Performance

	Proportion speaking time	Humorous comments	Mean Laughter Scale (1-5)	Change in print media coverage	Change in radio-TV coverage	Change in FEC contributions	Change in FEC contributors
Biden	.106	1.000	.300	16.667	300.667	211544.33	144.00
Clinton	.157	1.333	1.667	27.333	169.000	1628417.81	3590.00
Dodd	.104	.667	1.333	-.667	64.333	207846.73	153.67
Edwards	.140	.000	.000	85.333	419.333	414586.26	483.67
Gravel	.075	3.333	2.389	16.000	65.333	6618.03	15.33
Kucinich	.104	.333	1.000	12.000	204.667	3312.17	8.67
Obama	.175	1.333	2.000	75.667	261.333	595786.64	1543.33
Richardson	.139	1.000	2.000	17.667	208.667	190593.16	128.67

Audience response to the presidential candidates in terms of laughter was tested using two variables. One variable considers the number of humorous comments made and responded to by the audience during each debate, whereas the second variable considers average strength of audience response.[c] Only those instances where audience laughter occurred were used here.

Audience laughter intensity was coded on a five point scale, anchored by Barely Audible (1) for when the coder can barely distinguish audience laughter, followed by Slightly Audible (2), Moderately Audible (3), Very Audible (4), and Extremely Audible (5).[d] The average intensity of all comments during the debate under consideration is then used as a proxy for audience response.

Debate influence on mass media coverage and financial support
When change in print media from five days prior to and the period five days after the debates is compared, we see a significant change with an average change of 23.63 additional mentions of candidate names (SD=31.66).[e] Coverage by radio-television likewise significantly increased after the debates, as the average change in candidate mentions increased by an average of 214.52 (SD=242.52).[f] Therefore, we find support for the assertion that debates increase mass media coverage.

Change in individual financial support as a result of the presidential primary debates showed mixed results. Specifically, while the average amount of money given to candidates increased by $171,417.50 (SD=$870,662.43), the change only approached significance.[g] On the other hand, there was a significant increase in the numbers of individuals giving contributions as an average of 211.83 additional contributors gave as a result of the debates (SD=715.10).[h]

These findings provide partial support for the argument that debates increase individual financial participation.

Table 3.2: Descriptive statistics

Parameter	Mean	Standard Deviation
Change in print coverage	23.630	31.658
Change in radio-TV coverage	214.519	242.522
Change in total FEC contributions	171417.510	870662.430
Change in total FEC contributors	211.833	715.097
Proportion speaking time	.111	.035
Humorous comments made	1.241	1.273
Laughter intensity	1.594	1.394

Defining front-runner and long-shot candidates

Analysis of whether there was an appreciable effect in terms of media coverage and individual financial support based upon status as front-runner or long-shot was carried out by identifying those candidates that were high-profile before the electoral season began. Namely, for the Republican Party Rudy Giuliani, John McCain and Mitt Romney were particularly high profile, whereas Hillary Clinton, John Edwards and Barack Obama were media lights for the Democratic Party. With this in mind, and with all other candidates defined as second-tier candidates, differences in media treatment and financial support are tested.

Findings suggest that, while significant differences occur for both print media[i] and radio-TV[j] in the five days prior to the debates. Specifically, when the debates are grouped together, the six front-runners average 141.61 (SD=113.35) name mentions compared with a paltry 17.67 (SD=23.81) name mentions for the twelve long-shot candidates. This divide likewise can be seen with television and radio coverage, as front-runners average 523.44 (SD=302.11) name mentions, whereas second-tier candidates average 72.75 (SD=163.11) name mentions in the five days prior to the debates.

When considering proportion of time front-runners receive to speak during the debates, we find the same pattern occurs, albeit not as pronounced. There is a significant difference in speaking time during the debates based upon status.[k] Specifically, while long-shots are given an average of 9.36 percent of speaking time (SD=2.36), front-running candidates are given nearly 15 percent of the available speaking time (M=14.62; SD=2.75). Therefore, we see substantial support for the assertion that the mass media will focus on front-running candidates regardless of the electoral timing and the media format.

A similar pattern is found when individual Federal Elections Commission (FEC) contributions are considered. For both total dollars received and number of contributors in the five days prior to the debate we see that differences between front-runners and long-shot candidates show highly significant differences for both total FEC dollars received[l] and total contributors.[m] Here we find that front-runners receive an average of $845,666.64 dollars in the five days prior to debates (SD=$628,667.58) from 1072.11 contributors (SD=841.34), compared with long-shot candidates who received a meager $58,777.26 (SD=$100,727.15) from an average of 84.44 contributors (SD=130.00). Therefore, we find high levels of support for the assertion that front-runners will receive higher levels of individual support, likely due to their high profile position.

Table 3.3: Change in name mentions in the media (five days prior to five days after debate)

Parameter	Print media (log10)	Print media (log10)	Radio-TV (log10)	Radio-TV (log10)
Front-runner	-.468***	-.430**	-.368**	-.357**
# Humorous comments	.300*		.097	
Laughter strength		.141		.084
F-statistic	9.341***	6.361**	3.953*	3.883*
Adjusted R^2	.239	.168	.100	.098

†=significant at .10 level; *=significant at .05; **=significant at .01; ***=significant at .001

The effect of status and humor on coverage and contributions

Analysis of the effect of status and humor on change in the transformed variable measuring print media coverage suggests status has a significant and negative effect on name mentions,[n] an effect that remains stable across both equations (see Table 3.3).[o, p] However, of the two humor variables, only number of humorous comments exerts a significant, positive and moderately powerful effect on name mentions in the print media. The equations considering change in radio and television coverage likewise suggests there is a moderately strong and negative role played by candidate status, whereas neither number of humorous comments nor laughter strength plays a significant role. Therefore, while partial support is found for there being increased media coverage based upon candidates making more humorous comments that the audience responds to during each debate, there is not support for the assertion concerning the effect of audience laughter strength on increasing media coverage. Furthermore, counterintuitive findings are indicated with decreased coverage for front-runners.

Table 3.4: Change in Federal Elections Commission contributions (five days prior to five days after debate)

Parameter	FEC total contributions	FEC total contributions	FEC total contributors	FEC total contributors
Front-runner	-.028	-.039	-.014	-.020
# Humorous comments	-.028		.005	
Laughter strength		.200		.267†
F-statistic	.047	1.055	.004	1.879
Adjusted R^2	-.039	.002	-.041	.033

†=significant at .10 level; *=significant at .05; **=significant at .01; ***=significant at .001

On the other hand, change in financial support from prior to the debates to after the debates does not appear to have been affected by candidate status, whether front-runner or second-tier, or candidate humor, whether in the form of humorous comments made or the strength of audience laughter (see Table 3.4). Specifically, neither equations for total contributions to individual candidates nor the number of people giving contributions are significantly affected by candidate tier or humor during the debates.[9]

Discussion

The first finding is perhaps the most important finding, that debates do make a difference in both the print media and in radio and television mentions of individual candidates. Additionally, debates positively influence the number of individuals making financial contributions, if not total contributions made. Therefore, it appears that the initial debates provide salient events for those who cover politics for the mass media, as well as those individuals involved and motivated to make a difference in the process by giving money to individual candidates. The question remains as to whether the attention given during these initial debates was maintained throughout the course of the primary campaign season with its over forty debates punctuating the media landscape, or whether there was a level of fatigue that set in.

The next finding is that media attention begets media attention, with greater time given to candidates to respond to questions during the televised presidential primary debates leading to greater media coverage in the days following the debate. Indeed, when media coverage prior to debates is considered, one is led to the conclusion that media coverage is a self-perpetuating cycle, with a moderately high correlation between pre-debate coverage and time given to the candidates to respond during their debates.

Furthermore, the data analyzed here suggests the media selects and perpetuates front-runners and long-shot candidates. Here, according to Donovan and Hunsaker[9] the news media does not necessarily having strong incentives to "set expectations correctly" (p. 50). On the other hand, debates appear to provide a situation where media coverage of the front-runners is diminished in favor of long-shot candidates. In other words, although second-tier candidates may increase the amount of coverage they receive in relative terms, the front-runners maintain their dominance of coverage. In sum, the findings corroborate that of Donovan and Hunsaker, who in their analysis of primary elections from 1976-2008 found " . . . the media sets its own expectations and then voters *and* (emphasis theirs) the media responds to how candidate performance matches expectations" (p. 50).

During the early season debates, being able to induce audience laughter during the limited times in which the candidate has the floor appears to play a significant and positive role in print media coverage. Specifically, more humorous comments lead to more print coverage overall in terms of name mentions. However, average strength of audience laughter does not play a role in media coverage, nor does the number of laughter events or strength of audience laughter appear to influence radio and television coverage or financial support through FEC contributions.

Although humorous comments by the presidential candidates and audience laughter strength does not have the power expected, that does not mean that individual events in which there is an upwelling of emotion do not play "game-changing" roles. Media coverage of, and public reception towards such events as the Iowa caucus "Dean scream" by Howard Dean in 2004 and Hillary Clinton's upwelling of emotion prior to the New Hampshire primary in 2008, both in terms of her self-deprecating humorous comments during the New Hampshire debate and her nearly tearing up in the aftermath of her Iowa loss, can influence the viability of the candidates for good or ill. Furthermore, the nature of primary contests in which viable and "spoiler" candidates compete for camera time and media attention might cancel out the effect of humor. For instance, outsider candidate Alaska ex-Senator Mike Gravel used his camera time to attack his fellow Democratic Party candidates and, while he elicited hearty laughter from the audience, he signaled his position as a spoiler. Furthermore, Gravel's performance likely obviates that of Republican Party candidates John McCain and Mike Huckabee who regained and gained prominence, respectively, through the elicitation of audience laughter.

Conclusions

Although it appears that front-running candidates are established well prior to the primary elections, performance in early season primary debates plays a role in who survives and thrives as a presidential candidate. These early debates play a key role in defining for the public who is viable by first identifying how much attention each candidate receives.[9] In other words, more serious candidates receive greater amounts of airtime, which in turn determines the candidates more "deserving" of media attention. Second, audience response during debates, especially to humorous comments, can serve as a cue for who would be a more likely, indeed a better, leader by denoting an emotional connection between them. Specifically, those who make the most humorous comments are likely to receive greater print media coverage, especially early in the primary campaign when the serious contenders are still being identified.

An interesting corollary of the findings presented here is that it appears that the different news media cover debates differently.[12] Despite newspapers remaining an important source of political news, the increasing salience of the electronic media both through traditional television coverage and through the internet suggests future research should consider not just the quantity of coverage, but also the content of that coverage in both print and visual domains. Specifically, the electronic media with its visuals of the candidates has a far greater capacity to emotionally influence viewers.[23] As has been suggested by Pfau, Cho, and Chong[40] the new media, which includes such formats as political talk radio, television talk shows, entertainment shows, and television news magazines, exerts significant influence on public perception of presidential candidates. While not explicitly analyzing the initial stages of primary candidate impression formation, these new formats play a major role in voter choice, likely due to their ability to emotionally affect potential viewers.

As has been shown here, the influence of time spent viewing candidates, and experiencing the emotional response of the debates' audience, does have an influence on mass media coverage, and likely that of the public perceptions. However, caveats apply. The generalizability of the findings may be limited not just by the nature of the 2008 presidential campaign, which was unique in many important ways (although every campaign is unique in its own way), but also by the selection of debates to analyze. Although the selection was explicitly focused on those debates most likely to prime public perceptions, thus influencing electoral outcomes, it does not represent a random sampling of the over forty debates both parties engaged in during the 2008 presidential primary campaign. This, however, does not disguise the influence of attention and humor in winning over greater print media attention for presidential candidates.

Finally, humor is multi-faceted by nature, with multiple signaling properties. Not only does humor tell us something about the person making the humorous comment and the audience responding to the joke, it also has an effect on perceptions of the target. This chapter has focused solely on the positive aspects of humor through its ability to signal an emergent connection between the audience and the speaker and this connection's impact on the mass media covering the debates and individual contributors giving to the candidates; however it has not focused on the destructive aspects of humor. Humor used to ridicule other candidates may likewise have a negative impact on perceptions of and contributions to the target. Likewise, the inability of a candidate to respond well to a humorous comment, i.e., take a joke, may also harm that candidate's electoral prospects. In sum, much remains to be considered when humor by candidates is studied, with the following chapters exploring the nature of humor and laughter and its use by presidential candidates with the aim of providing a more complete picture.

Notes

[a] Status of candidates likely affects the perception of how humorous they are with those candidates perceived as having higher status and prestige more likely to be seen as humorous. This in turn leads to greater liking of the political figure making the humorous comment. Therefore, while it may be expected that presidential candidates with front-runner status making more humorous comments and eliciting louder laughter will reap the benefits of increased media coverage and individual financial support, statistical analysis of the first three debates for Republicans and Democrats did not show such an effect.

[b] Because I analyze change from pre- to post-debate, the model addresses concerns about seasonality with the data. In addition, I carried out a statistical diagnostic of the base equation, one in which I did not model seasonal interaction effects, and found the Durbin-Watson statistic to be well within the acceptable zone for all equations, suggesting no problem with autocorrelation.

[c] Data collection was initiated on the basis of laughter identification with two trained coders independently ascertaining when laughter occurred and then reaching consensus

as to the final inventory of laughter events. Next, a multi-stage process to identify the source of laughter and the strength of the laughter was carried out. Specifically, each coder was asked to identify who was laughing through the following stages: individual (candidate or moderator—by name if possible), then panel (if more than one individual candidate and/or moderator laughs), then audience. If the audience laughs, this code supersedes both individual and panel as the coding category.

[d] While microphones might not accurately reflect the intensity of the audience's response (due mainly to acoustics, but also the physical structure of the event, which might mute response), and hence the intensity of response might be misrepresented here, the perception of those viewing the debates are the same as the coders.

[e] Paired samples t-tests: $t[53]=5.485, p>.001$.

[f] Paired samples t-tests: $t[53]=6.500, p>.001$.

[g] Paired samples t-test, $t[53]=1.447, p=.154$.

[h] Paired samples t-test: $t[53]=2.177, p=.034$.

[i] Equal variances cannot be assumed: Levene test for print media $F=31.968, p>.001$; $t[17.754]=-4.589, p>.001$

[j] Equal variances cannot be assumed: Levene test for radio-television $F=16.990$, $p>.001$; $t[22.089], p>.001$.

[k] Levene test: $F=.870, p=.355$; $t[52]=-7.326, p>.001$.

[l] Levene test: $F=48.948, p>.001$; $t[17.438]=-5.277, p>.001$.

[m] Levene test: $F=55.992, p>.001$; $t[17.407]=-4.951, p>.001$.

[n] While it may be expected that humor and status are related, with long-shot candidates more likely to make humorous comments to make the most of their sparse media coverage or that front-runners are more likely to have their humor recognized and laughed at, independent samples t-tests, with equal variances assumed due to non-significant Levene tests (Humorous comment $F=2.470, p=.122$; Laughter strength $F=.032, p=.858$), there is no significant difference in the number of humorous comments made by front-runners and second tier candidates, $t=-1.060, p=.924$, or the strength of audience laughter elicited, $t=-.285, p=.777$.

[o] Due to extreme positive skewness in the distribution of media coverage and FEC contribution data, these variables were transformed with a log to the tenth power function. Next, change in the four variables was computed by subtracting coverage and contribution data in the five days prior to the debates from that of five days after the debates occurred. The resulting four variables do not exhibit the extreme skewness apparent in the untransformed variables, allowing the use of linear statistical analysis. In this case, ordinary least squares regression is used due to its robust nature. Additionally, due to concerns over collinearity between the number of humorous comments made (and responded to by the audience) and laughter strength, separate equations are run.

[p] All equations were run with political party as covariate (0=Republican Party debate; 1=Democratic Party debate). However, this variable did not reach significance in any of the equations.

[q] Although, as can be expected, relationships exist between change in print media and radio-television coverage, $r=.334, p=.013$, and between change in total FEC contributions and FEC contributors, $r=.876, p>.001$, there is no statistically significant relationship between change in media coverage and FEC contributions. Specifically, change in print media coverage shows no significant relationship with change in total FEC contributions, $r=.062, p=.661$, or with change in number of FEC individual contributors, $r=.170, p=.230$. Likewise, change in radio and television coverage has no significant

effect with change in total FEC money given, $r=-.010$, $p=.943$, nor with change in the number of contributors, $r=.066$, $p=.641$.

References

1. Racine Group. White paper on televised political campaign debates. *Argumentation and Advocacy 38*, 199-218 (2002).
2. Bucy, E. P. & Ball, J. Quantifying the claim that Nixon looked bad: A visual analysis of the Kennedy-Nixon debates. Indiana University, Bloomington, IN (2011).
3. Benoit, W. L. & Hansen, G. J. Presidential Debate Watching, Issue Knowledge, Character Evaluation, and Vote Choice. *Human Communication Research 30*, 121-144 (2004).
4. Benoit, W. L., McKinney, M. S. & Stephenson, M. T. Effects of Watching Primary Debates in the 2000 U.S. Presidential Campaign. *J. Commun. 52*, 316 (2002).
5. Lang, G. E. & Lang, K. Immediate and Delayed Responses to a Carter-Ford Debate: Assessing Public Opinion. *The Public Opinion Quarterly 42*, 322-341 (1978).
6. Vancil, D. L. & Pendell, S. D. Winning presidential debates: An analysis of criteria influencing audience response. *Western Journal of Communication 48*, 62-74 (1984).
7. Yawn, M., Ellsworth, K., Beatty, B. & Kahn, K. F. How a presidential primary debate changed attitudes of audience members. *Polit. Behav. 20*, 155-181 (1998).
8. Mutz, D. C. Effects of horse-race coverage on campaign coffers: Strategic contributing in presidential primaries. *The Journal of Politics 57*, 1015-1042 (1995).
9. Donovan, T. & Hunsaker, R. Beyond Expectations: Effects of Early Elections in U.S. Presidential Nomination Contests. *PS: Political Science & Politics 42*, 45-52 (2009).
10. Shaw, D. R. The Impact of News Media Favorability and Candidate Events in Presidential Campaigns. *Political Communication 16*, 183-202 (1999).
11. Shaw, D. R. & Roberts, B. E. Campaign Events, the Media and the Prospects of Victory: The 1992 and 1996 U.S. Presidential... *British Journal of Political Science 30*, 259 (2000).
12. Benoit, W. L., Stein, K. A. & Hansen, G. J. Newspaper Coverage of Presidential Debates. *Argumentation & Advocacy 41*, 17-27 (2004).
13. Jamieson, K. H. & Waldman, P. in *The press effect: politicians, journalists, and the stories that shape the political world* 220-220 (Oxford University Press, Oxford; New York, 2004).
14. Newton, J. S., Masters, R. D., McHugo, G. J. & Sullivan, D. G. Making up our minds: Effects of network coverage on viewer impressions of leaders. *Polity 20*, 226-246 (1987).

15. Norton, M. I. & Goethals, G. R. Spin (and pitch) doctors: Campaign strategies in televised political debates. *Polit. Behav. 26*, 227-248 (2004).
16. Damore, D. F. A dynamic model of candidate fundraising: The case of presidential nomination campaigns. *Political Research Quarterly 50*, 343-364 (1997).
17. Lanoue, D. J. & Schrott, P. R. The effects of primary season debates on public opinion. *Polit. Behav. 11*, 289-306 (1989).
18. Pfau, M. *et al*. Influence of communication during the distant phase of the 1996 Republican presidential primary campaign. *J. Commun. 47*, 6-26 (1997).
19. Chance, M. R. A. Attention Structure as the Basis of Primate Rank Orders. *Man 2*, 503-518 (1967).
20. Mazur, A. in *Biosociology of dominance and deference* (Rowman & Littlefield, Lanham, MD, 2005).
21. Salter, F. K. in *Emotions in command: Biology, bureaucracy, and cultural evolution* (Transaction Pub, New Brunswick, NJ, 2007).
22. Hatfield, E., Cacioppo, J. T. & Rapson, R. L. in *Emotional contagion (studies in emotion & social interaction)* 240 (Cambridge University Press, New York, NY, 1994).
23. Grabe, M. E. & Bucy, E. P. in *Image bite politics: news and the visual framing of elections* 316 (Oxford University Press, Oxford; New York, 2009).
24. Masters, R. D. in *The nature of politics* 298 (Yale University Press, New Haven, 1989).
25. Haslam, S. A., Reicher, S. D. & Platow, M. J. in *The new psychology of leadership: Identity, influence and power* 296 (Psychology Press, New York, NY, 2010).
26. Van Vugt, M. & Ahuja, A. in *Naturally selected: The evolutionary science of leadership* 272 (Harper Collins, New York, NY, 2011).
27. Brader, T. in *Campaigning for hearts and minds: How emotional appeals in political ads work* (University Of Chicago Press, Chicago, IL, 2006).
28. Marcus, G. E., Neuman, W. R. & MacKuen, M. in *Affective intelligence and political judgment* (University of Chicago Press, Chicago, IL, 2000).
29. Eibl-Eibesfeldt, I. in *Human ethology* 848 (Aldine De Gruyter, New York, 1989).
30. Masters, R. D., Sullivan, D. G., Lanzetta, J. T., McHugo, G. J. & Englis, B. G. The facial displays of leaders: Toward an ethology of human politics. *J. Soc. Biol. Struct. 9*, 319-343 (1986).
31. Sullivan, D. G. & Masters, R. D. 'Happy Warriors': Leaders' Facial Displays, Viewers' Emotions, and Political Support. *Am. J. Polit. Sci. 32*, 345-368 (1988).
32. House, R. J., Spangler, W. D. & Woycke, J. Personality and charisma in the U.S. presidency: A psychological theory of leader effectiveness. *Adm. Sci. Q. 36* (1991).

33. Schubert, J. N., Stewart, P. A. & Curran, M. A. A defining presidential moment: 9/11 and the rally effect. *Polit. Psychol. 23*, 559-583 (2002).
34. Stewart, P. A., Waller, B. M. & Schubert, J. N. Presidential speechmaking style: Emotional response to micro-expressions of facial affect. *Motiv. Emotion 33*, 125-135 (2009).
35. Henrich, J. & Gil-White, F. J. The evolution of prestige: Freely conferred deference as a mechanism for enhancing the benefits of cultural transmission. *Evolution and Human Behavior 22*, 165-196 (2001).
36. Patterson, M. L., Churchill, M. E., Burger, G. K. & Powell, J. L. Verbal and nonverbal modality effects on impressions of political candidates: Analysis from the 1984 presidential debates. *Communication Monographs 59*, 231-242 (1992).
37. Way, B. M. & Masters, R. D. Political attitudes: Interactions of cognition and affect. *Motivation & Emotion 20*, 205 (1996).
38. Weisfeld, G. E. *et al.* Do women seek humorousness in men because it signals intelligence? A cross-cultural test. *Humor–International Journal of Humor Research* (Forthcoming).
39. Haynes, A. A. & Pitts, B. Making an Impression: New Media in the 2008 Presidential Nomination Campaigns. *PS: Political Science & Politics 42*, 53-58 (2009).
40. Pfau, M., Cho, J. & Chong, K. Communication Forms in U.S. Presidential Campaigns: Influences on Candidate Perceptions and the Democratic Process. *Harvard International Journal of Press/Politics 6*, 88 (2001).

Chapter 4
Punchline Politics:
Laughter and Humor during Primary Debates

Humor has long been valued for its ability to convey qualities about politicians to the public, both when the politicians define themselves[1-3] and when the politicians are defined by others, whether by contending candidates[1, 2, 4, 5] or by the media.[6-14] And by virtue of humorous comments being pithy encapsulations, they can reverberate long after they were originally uttered, elevating the status of the joke teller while defining the target. Furthermore, by making individuals laugh, politicians develop emotional connections with potential supporters.

The connection between candidates and their followers in the form of audience laughter provides insight into their dialogue in terms of the message presented and the resonance it has. A candidate capable of eliciting audience laughter, especially in a competitive setting such as debates, has arguably established a strong emotional connection with the audience. At the same time, depending on the nature of the humorous comments, this connection may enhance the mutual bond between the candidates and the audience while at the same time creating distance between the audience and the candidate's opponent(s). While debates tend mainly to reinforce candidate and policy preferences,[15-19] these debates and the impressions individual candidates leave still have the potential to sway the opinions of undecided voters,[18, 20] as well as motivate supporters to turn out at the polls. The influence debates have is further accentuated by post-debate press analyses that not only establish immediate winners and losers, but also a candidate's long-term electoral viability.[20-23]

Humor, whether used by candidates to attack competitors and outsiders while not appearing impolite,[24] or used to signal both high levels of prestige between the candidate and the audience and the candidate's willingness and ability to reduce this divide through self-deprecatory humor,[25-29] depends on audience laughter to signal its success.[30] In addition to enhancing the candidate's status and connection with the audience and the press, humor can reduce scrutiny and critical argument of assertions made[14, 31] while enhancing discussion and most likely, press coverage.[30, 32] Candidates, regardless of their position in the race, benefit as a result of their successful utilization of humor and the laughter that occurs. However, the type and amount of humorous comments might differ depending on whether the candidate is a front-runner or a second-tier candidate.

Two examples from the 2008 primary debates stand out. The first occurred during the second Republican debate on 15 May 2007 in South Carolina and established former Arkansas governor Mike Huckabee's position as more than just a fringe candidate. During the debates, when he was asked about federal spending, Huckabee elevated himself while derogating Democratic Party candidate John Edwards by stating "We've had a Congress that has spent money like Edwards at a beauty shop." Through this quip, Huckabee was able to establish himself as a crowd favorite by eliciting the longest, and arguably strongest, audience response for all the debates considered in terms of both laughter (twelve seconds) and laughter-then-applause (twenty-two seconds). Substantively, the humorous comment enabled him to metaphorically "kill two birds with one stone" as he shared encrypted knowledge with the audience. First, it established Huckabee as an outsider to Washington politics, where the Republican Party under President George W. Bush and a Republican Congress had been characterized as engaging in wasteful spending by the moderator's question. At the same time Huckabee attacked a front-running presidential opponent from the opposing party who had positioned himself as the populist candidate for not living up to the same standards due to his paying $400 for a haircut. Essentially, Edwards was a flip-flopper. But perhaps most appreciable, Huckabee skewered Edward's masculinity by juxtaposing his name with the term "beauty shop" playing upon Republican Party norms of manliness and staying the course. In sum, Huckabee established his bona fides as a Washington outsider and as a populist candidate, while enhancing his popular and media appeal at the expense of an out-group candidate.[33, 34]

A second example occurred later in the campaign during the Democratic Party debate just before the 2008 New Hampshire primary. Here, Hillary Clinton, stinging from Barack Obama's staggering victory in the Iowa caucuses and needing a win to re-establish herself as a front-running candidate, was able to use self-deprecating humor to humanize herself and make herself more likeable to the public.[34, 35] Specifically, when asked about New Hampshire poll findings that she was respected but not liked as much as Obama, Clinton responded with feigned distress "Well . . . that hurts my feelings" and smiled and sighed in mock resignation. This elicited seven seconds of humor-then-applause. She then further worked the crowd through the mock-melodramatic response, "But I'll try to go on." This received four seconds of laughter, Clinton then received another brief laugh (one second) for stating "I don't think I'm that bad." The icing on the cake, however, came when Obama, not playing along by not looking at her directly or smiling, countered "You're likeable enough, Hillary, no doubt about it" to which Clinton answered "Thank you so much" while smiling broadly and shifting her head and body in apparent delight, eliciting four further seconds of laughter from the audience. This response managed to reverse the positions of both candidates in terms of their likeability, as Clinton's response effectively warmed her tough persona while Obama's rejoinder made him appear cold. In the primary three days later, Clinton achieved a surprise victory over Obama, who in some polls had a double digit lead, due in no small part to her being more emotionally accessible.[a]

As can be seen, humor, and the laughter indicating its success, during debates does make a difference in how candidates are seen as performing both by the audience and the media. It arguably can be seen as elevating prestige and increasing attention, important goals for any candidate. This chapter systematically explores the nature of audience laughter and its elicitation by presidential candidates and moderators during ten 2008 primary debates. Applause and laughter indicate both audience support and level of social contagion.[36] Specifically, laughter shows both support for the source of the humorous comment and (potentially) ostracism of its target.[37] Due to a lack of quantitative research concerning political humor over the course of a campaign, this chapter evaluates how Republican and Democratic presidential candidates use humor during primary debates and audience reaction to them.[b] This chapter then considers the role of candidate status as front-runner or second-tier on the target of humorous comments and audience response before drawing conclusions.

Humor on the campaign trail

Comments with humorous intent are often made by presidential candidates; the litmus test of the effectiveness of a humorous comment is its ability to elicit laughter in the listening audience. However, not all humorous comments will extract audience laughter; some comments might elicit laughter from fellow candidates or the moderators, or might just highlight comments by the speaker.[38, 39] Furthermore, whether or not such comments actually are "humorous" is open to dispute due to the contextual as well as the highly subjective and interpersonal nature of humor.[38, 40-42] In the former, a response to a question about President George W. Bush's infamous political handler in the first Republican Party debate by Virginia governor Jim Gilmore in which he elicited laughter from the panel by commenting "What's important to this nation is not Karl Rove" may be seen as a highly encrypted in-joke concerning Rove's political influence that was appreciated by fellow candidates, but likely was too obscure for the audience. In the case of the latter, candidates may laugh to themselves while they are speaking due to self-perceived incongruities. For instance, when Barack Obama responded to a question concerning his lack of experience during the Super Tuesday debate by commenting "Let me ah, let me just also point out that, ah, Mitt Romney hasn't gotten a very good return on his investment during this presidential campaign (audience laughter). I'm happy to take a look at my management style (Obama laughter) during the course of this last year and his. I think they compare fairly well (audience laughter)" he apparently reflected upon an incongruous comparison and "laughed off" a perceived weakness, along with a supportive audience. Therefore, what can be expected is that due to the social nature of political debates, candidates will attempt to reflect the norms and values of the audience through their attempts at humor whereas the audience will in turn show their understanding and support through laughter.

Humor and laughter are substantially coupled, with laughter often seen as indicating successful humor. Laughter, like smiling, is predominantly a social behavior, both of which are, in the words of Robert Provine[43] ". . . acts that are either evoked by or performed primarily in the presence of other individuals" (p. 158).[c] Furthermore, the quality of the laugh might affect its contagiousness[44, 45], [d] with individual and group ties consolidated and cemented by laughter.[36, 46] Laughter, both by its contagiousness and by its character, signals emotional intent and may be differentiated into the socially affiliative properties of joy and happiness or competitive qualities of taunt and contempt.[47]

Although laughter is typically associated with positive emotions, due mainly to the "play face" typically accompanying it (see chapter 5), and is highly contagious, evidence suggests it does not necessarily reflect the internal state of the laughing individual. Instead, laughter serves as a means of indicating assent within a group and coordinating large group activity. Devereux and Ginsburg[46] suggest positive emotions and laughter may be decoupled as respondent laughter and their happiness and amusement were not related. Furthermore, while size of audience in Devereux and Ginsburg's study played a significant and positive role, as expected, there was greater frequency and longer duration of laughter when strangers, as opposed to friends, interacted with each other. This suggests that laughter serves a social signaling role indicating shared norms,[40, 41, 48] a finding supported by research by Michael Platow and colleagues that shows perceived in-group or out-group composition of a laughing audience influences respondent laughter, smiling and professed humorousness of material.[49] It may also be used to enforce in-group/out-group boundaries through "jeering"/"mobbing" behavior, in which there is a synchronized group response to drive intruders away.[50]

The size of the audience likewise affects the amount of laughter, with greater laughter coming from larger audiences,[45] although an individual does not need to be physically present to be affected by laughter due to its contagious character.[36, 45, 51] This laughter from individuals or an audience may serve to show respect to the speaker. Here, in the words of Irenäus Eibl-Eibesfeldt[50] "(R)espect is shown in self-deprecation, often regressing into infantilisms, giggling, laughing, and appearing to be helpless" (p. 508). Due to the relaxed open-mouth "play face" being evident in laughing individuals, one may conclude that there is an absence of aggressive intent and a willingness, even a desire to, affiliate.[52, 53]

As politics is ultimately a group activity, with individuals competing within the group to attain and maintain power, and successful groups out-competing and/or co-opting other contending groups, the ability to out-mobilize and out-coordinate other groups is of the greatest importance and is contingent on the ability of followers to communicate their agreement with each other and their leader.[41] Laughter, by communicating positive feelings and support provides just such a method of assent. The political party, and ultimately the candidate, most capable of eliciting positive emotional response from greater numbers of people are more likely to be successful.[54]

A major goal of humor is uniting group members against both internal and external threats. Humor, when marked by laughter, identifies who belongs to a group, often doing so at the expense of transgressors on group values. In the words of Frank Salter,[53] "(L)aughter, especially from a group, can be a devastating weapon of intimidation. It signals simultaneously the group's designation of the target as of low status and the mutual affiliation of the group to the exclusion of the target" (p. 365). Through this focus on "ideological invaders," humor and concomitant laughter likely represents symbolic attacks on those breaking with the norms of the group.[37, 50, 55-56]

Furthermore, in addition to directly targeting those breaking group norms, Janes and Olson[57] found that the audiences of humor that ridiculed an individual were more likely to conform to group behavior expectations.

Politics likely presents an attenuated case of group norm enforcement, as competing and hostile groups and individuals attempt to form coalitions against each other for control of the "spoils" within a larger encompassing group. In societies that are more egalitarian and democratic, such as the United States, political competition for the spoils (who gets what, where, and when) does not take the form of actual physical coercive activities; instead it takes on the form of verbal (and nonverbal) competition, with the leader of each coalition attempting to gain political control through the use of masterful rhetoric to win votes and elections. Specifically, political humor allows its practitioners to attack opponents, belittling them and/or the positions they hold, while appearing to create "acceptable" hostility and reinforcing it toward the targeted group.[24, 58] With in-group humor, the comments are expected to strengthen ties between the candidate and the audience by reducing anxiety when laughter is elicited. In essence, politicians using humor to evoke audience laughter focus and coordinate the audience's affective response while strengthening group bonds and loyalty.[59, 60]

Therefore, in debates the targets of humor ought to range from the *out-group*, in which case attacking humor would be used, to the *in-group*, whereas the humor ought to be playful, and finally to *non-aligned individuals*, as candidates likely will want to either be playful with or, at the very least, want to avoid alienating these potential converts. In the first group, the out-group, the targets of humor will be those individuals and organizations which are agreed-upon enemies of the audience being spoken to. For instance, when Mitt Romney made the comment "The only thing I can think of that would be as bad as that would to have, the the gang of three running the war on terror—Pelosi, Reid, and Hillary Clinton" during the first Republican Party debate, he targeted the three most visible and powerful Democratic Party leaders, Speaker of the House Nancy Pelosi, Senate Majority Leader Harry Reid, and then presidential front-runner Hillary Clinton for his attack.

Additionally, competitors may be considered as part of this group as the speaker will want to alienate his/her audience from other candidates and ally the audience behind themselves through the use of humor. This appeared to the strategy of Democratic Party long-shot candidate Mike Gravel throughout his campaign, as he targeted other Democratic candidates with acerbic humor, including his shot in the first debate when he said "It's like going into the Senate, you know, the first time you get there you're excited—my god how did I ever get here, then about six months later you say, how the hell did the rest of them get here?" In sum, as political humor tends to disparage the opposition more often than not, it is expected that competitors and out-groups will bear the brunt of humorous comments in these debates.

As political humor concerns itself with disparaging other groups and/or strengthening the ties between individuals within a group, it is highly probable that political party plays a role in the target of such humorous comments and, potentially, to audience response. Specifically, as the Republican and Democratic parties have differentiated themselves in not only their policy positions, but also their level of inclusiveness and hierarchy,[61, 62] differences in the brunt of jokes can be expected. Due to the Republican Party establishing itself as a strongly hierarchical group that is more likely to employ party discipline to "patrol" its borders, even to the point of defining itself by who it excludes, we expect Republican candidates to be more likely to focus their humor on the out-group in comparison with the Democratic Party. For example, when long-shot Republican Party candidate Duncan Hunter made the comment "I think the guy with, who's got the most influence right here with these three gentlemen is Ted Kennedy (laughter) and I think we need to move away from the Kennedy wing of the Republican Party" he attempted to define front-runners Mitt Romney, Rudy Giuliani and John McCain as being in league with the opposition and thus traitorous to the in-group. Additionally, as laughter might be seen as indicating group cohesion, it might be further expected that length and strength of audience laughter might differ based upon political party. Specifically, the more unified and hierarchical Republican Party will likely elicit longer and stronger audience laughter than the more diffusely organized Democratic Party.

The in-group is an inclusive group, although it may be subdivided further. Specifically, the in-group may include supporters not present and those that are actually present in the audience. In addition, the moderators are non-aligned individuals who may, by virtue of interacting with the contending candidates, be the target of humorous comments. In all these cases, it is expected humor will be more affiliative and playful as was the case when a deadpan Joe Biden responded to moderator Brian Williams query "(Williams) Senator Biden, words have in the past gotten you in trouble, words that were borrowed and words that some found hateful. An editorial in the Los Angeles Times said in addition to his uncontrolled verbosity Biden is a gaffe machine. Can you reassure voters in this country that you would have the discipline you would need on the world stage senator?" to which Biden responded with a simple "Yes" eliciting audience laughter and a very subtle yet telling "tongue show" by Williams before he sardonically commented "Thank you Senator Biden." Finally, the speaker him/herself, as well as his/her family, may be the focus of humorous comments. However, it is fully expected these jibes will be more affiliative and non-threatening.

In both the case of humorous comments directed toward the in-group or the out-group, the prestige of the individual performing the humorous comment is enhanced by inducing audience laughter.[42, 63-66] Specifically, the speaker displays dominance by attaining and maintaining attention[50, 53, 67, 68] and signals cognitive mastery and status by making humorous comments at the expense of others.[27, 37, 69, e] Perhaps most importantly, the candidate is the focal point in distinguishing and enforcing group norms. Furthermore, if there is a long-standing relationship between the speaker and the target, this increased familiarity likely leads to interpretation of humor as pro-social.[66] Thus, candidates who use humor effectively can bolster their prestige and strengthen their bond with the in-group.

The status and prestige of candidates, in other words, their rank within a group and the level of social esteem they are held in, likely will influence both the amount of humorous comments they make and on whom these comments are targeted. Front-runners, because they already have the attention of the press and the public, likely will not need to attain attention through humor, when compared with their second-tier compatriots who will work hard to obtain this attention. It is thus expected fewer humorous comments will be made by front-running candidates when compared to second-tier candidates. Further, these front-running candidates will likely want to underscore their status and prestige by making comments which reduce the divide between the leader and followers. These comments will likely either underscore the leader's "conspicuous consumption" of prestige, or focus on their close and relaxed connections with the audience and the in-group which allows for them to make such comments without worrying that the strength of that relationship will be diminished.[50] On the other hand, second-tier candidates, in addition to making more humorous comments, will likely disparage the out-group and competitors to lower their target's prestige, while raising their own. Therefore, it is expected that front-running candidates will focus their humorous comments on the in-group, whereas second-tier candidates will make more humorous comments targeting the out-group.

It is also expected that the laughter itself will be influenced by the status of the candidate making the humorous comment. Specifically, front-running candidates, with their greater status and higher levels of prestige in comparison to second-tier candidates, will more likely elicit stronger laughter in terms of numbers of individuals laughing as well as the length and strength of laughter. This is expected due to front-runners attaining and maintaining higher levels of attention[50, 53, 67, 68] and being more capable of eliciting congruent display behavior.[70]

The 2008 presidential primary debates

The ten presidential primary debates considered were comprised of the initial three presidential debates for each political party then the back-to-back Republican then Democratic Party debates the night prior to the New Hampshire primary and Super Tuesday (see Box 1.1) and are analyzed in the aggregate. Data collection was initiated on the basis of laughter identification with this information providing the basis for identifying the source and the target of humorous comments. The source of the humorous comment is then coded on the basis of them being a moderator or a presidential candidate, and if a candidate, on the basis of their political party. Of the 319 cases considered, the moderators accounted for 31.3 percent of all humorous comments, whereas the Republican and Democratic Party candidates accounted for 39.8 percent and 28.8 percent of humorous comments, respectively. Here I focus solely on utterances by candidates of the two parties.

Table 4.1: Descriptive statistics

Variable		Republican Party	Democratic Party	Total
Debate number	#1	31.2%	11.2%	22.3%
	#2	11.9%	18.9%	15.0%
	#3	11.4%	11.2%	11.3%
	#4	27.3%	25.2%	26.3%
	#5	18.2%	33.6%	25.1%
Target of humorous	Speaker	8.0%	13.5%	10.5%
comment	Family	0.0%	4.3%	1.9%
	In-group	14.4%	5.7%	10.5%
	Moderator	8.0%	9.2%	8.6%
	Audience	2.3%	0.7%	1.6%
	Competitor	48.9%	58.9%	53.3%
	Out-group	10.2%	3.5%	13.7%

The target of the humorous comment is identified as focusing on either the speaker, the speaker's family, the speaker's in-group, the moderator, the audience, a competitor, or the speaker's out-group. Analysis of the target of humorous comments suggests that nearly two-thirds of all humorous comments eliciting audience laughter focused on the competition (see Figure 4.1). Specifically, over half of humorous comments focused on competitors for the presidency, while just over 13 percent focused on the out-groups to the competitors and the audience. Humor focused on the in-group in a much smaller proportion of total comments, with just about 10 percent considering the in-group that was not present, and nearly a paltry 2.5 percent focused on the audience. This is likely due to the lack of direct interaction with the audience during the debate, as 8 percent of humorous comments focused on the moderators of the debates. Finally, self-referential humor made up nearly 13 percent of humorous comments, while comments focusing on the candidate's family consisted of nearly 3 percent of the total. For the sake of statistical analysis, and due to theoretical rationales stated above, humor focused on competitors and out-groups are combined into "out-group" while humorous comments about the speaker, the speaker's family, the audience, the moderator and other in-group members are combined into "in-group."

Next, a multi-stage process identified the source, length and strength of laughter. Findings concerning the source of laughter suggest audience laughter predominated, with over two-thirds (67.7 percent) of the cases emanating from them. Of the remainder, one-fifth (22.6 percent) of all laughter events derive from individual candidates and moderators, while nearly 10 percent came from the panel as a whole (9.7 percent). Considering the laughter of individual candidates, we see that it derived chiefly from three candidates: Mitt Romney in nearly one-third (29.1 percent) of the cases in which individuals laughed followed by Hillary Clinton who laughed one-fifth of the total (20.8 percent) while John McCain nearly matched her total (19.4 percent of the time).[f]

Figure 4.1: Target of humorous comments

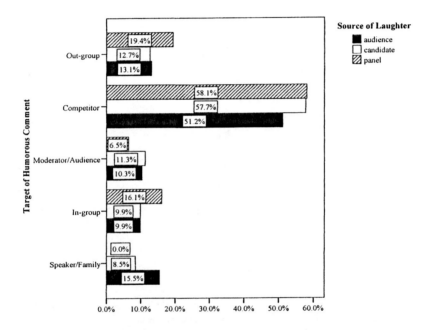

Laughter onset time was noted, as was its cessation, and was rounded to the second. In those times when audience laughter dissolved into applause, the laughter offset was estimated, and the applause end was noted as a separate variable. Scrutiny of the length of the laughter events for all 319 cases suggests laughter lasted for a relatively short period of time, just over two seconds, and exhibited relatively little variance at just over a second and a half (M=2.17s; SD=1.67s). For those events in which audience laughter alone was considered (N=216), the results were highly comparable (M=2.46s; SD=1.75s), albeit slightly longer. Finally, those events in which audience applause followed laughter occurred in thirty-five cases and averaged about eight seconds (M=7.83s; SD=4.82s).

The next stage of coding classified audience laughter intensity. Due to laughter by individual candidates and moderators being amplified by proximity to their microphones, only audience laughter is coded. A five-point scale ranging from Barely Audible (1), whereas the coder can barely distinguish audience laughter, to Extremely Audible (5) in which the laughter is at its loudest, is used.[g] Findings suggest average audience laughter being slightly-to-moderately audible (M=2.36; SD=1.15).

Figure 4.2: Average laughter time due to candidate humor

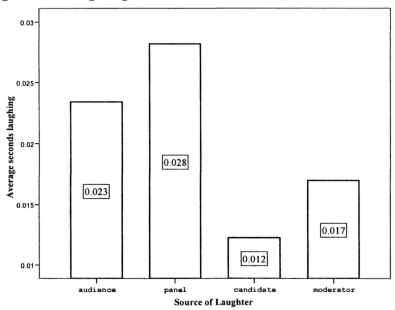

Political party

Laughter occurred during each of the debates, albeit at different levels. All told, the 319 laughter-eliciting events were roughly evenly interspersed between the two political parties. Once moderator humor was removed, there were significant differences in the patterns in which laughter was elicited in the remaining 219 cases.[h] Specifically, while the first Republican debate accounted for nearly one-quarter of all laughter, then diminished for the next two debates before picking up steam in the last two debates, the first three Democratic Party debates were comparatively sparse in the amount of laughter events when compared with the New Hampshire and Super Tuesday events (see Table 4.1) which accounted for over one-quarter and one-third of all humorous comments, respectively.

Analysis of the target of humorous comments on the basis of political party the candidates belong to suggests there are no significant differences between them.[i] Therefore, in the 218 humorous comments made by presidential candidates of both political parties, we find no statistical support for the assertion that Republican candidates will focus their humor more on the out-group than Democratic Party candidates.

The best way to compare across political parties, given the variation in candidate participation both in the number of debates and the amount of time given them to speak, is to standardize by dividing minutes spoken (converted to a 100 point scale) by humorous comments during the five respective debates for the Republicans and Democrats. However, when the number of humorous comments told per minute by each candidate was considered, significant differences between the two parties assert itself.[j] Here, Republican Party candidates make humorous comments once every three minutes (M=3.15; SD=3.13), compared with the Democratic Party candidates who make a humorous comment nearly every six minutes (M=5.97; SD=4.11). While party differences are apparent with this finding, and provide tangential support for the assertion that Republicans use more humor, this finding is likely related to the number of candidates taking part in each debate. Specifically, the Republican race was wide open with ten candidates at the start, ending with six and four candidates taking part in the last two races, respectively; in comparison, the Democratic Party primaries started with eight candidates, then narrowed down to four and two candidates in the last two debates. As discussed later, it can be expected that more candidates will lead to more competition for attention, and thus greater use of humor.

Examination of differences between the Republican and Democratic parties based upon length and strength of audience laughter suggests no significant differences in judged laughter strength, although length of laughter approaches significant differences. Specifically, differences between the two parties only approached significance with the Republican Party audiences laughing slightly longer (M=2.58 seconds; SD=1.63) than Democratic Party audiences (M=2.14s; SD=1.36).[k] However, when events in which laughter was followed by applause are considered, there are no significant differences between the political parties.[l] Finally, there were no significant differences between the two parties concerning strength of laughter.[m] Therefore, we find only slight support for the Republican Party eliciting longer and stronger audience laughter, as audience laughter for Republican candidates only approached being significantly longer.

Front-runners vs. second-tier candidates

Although front-runners and second-tier candidates can be prima facie identified as such by the tone, tenor and tempo of media coverage, corroboration can be seen in systematic analysis of multiple indicators. As shown in the previous chapter, name mentions of the candidates in print media and radio-television and the amount of money each candidate received in individual contributions, all in the five days prior to the debate under consideration provide corroboration of their status. To a lesser extent, the proportion of speaking time during each debate reflects the electoral status of the respective candidates. Here, the initial three debates of each political party provide the basis for our analysis. This is due to the latter two debates under consideration (New Hampshire and Super Tuesday) seeing the great majority of "also-rans" winnowed out.

For the Republican party, New York City Mayor Rudy Giuliani, Arizona Senator John McCain and Massachusetts Governor Mitt Romney stand out as front-runners from the field of ten candidates, although in the early debates Texas Congressman Ron Paul's insurgent brand of libertarian-Republicanism won him substantial print-media coverage and a larger proportion of debate speaking time in the second Republican debate hosted by Fox News (see Table 4.2a). However, in terms of radio and television coverage and size of FEC contributions, Paul, along with the other Republican candidates, was dwarfed by "Rudy McRomney." Therefore, these three were defined as front-runners, with the other seven candidates (Brownback, Gilmore, Huckabee, Hunter, Paul, Tancredo, T. Thompson and F. Thompson) considered second-tier candidates.

While the early primary field for the Democratic Party held two fewer candidates, a similar pattern emerged. Here New York Senator Hillary Clinton, ex-Vice Presidential candidate John Edwards, and Illinois Senator Barack Obama received the most attention and money (Table 4.3b). Although the third debate, hosted by PBS, saw greater equality in time given to all candidates, the pattern of these three as front-runners is accentuated by the amount of radio-television media coverage and individual financial contributions received.

Differences between front-running and second-tier candidates in terms of humorous comments is considered through analysis of the variable "minutes per joke" computed on the basis of each candidate's performance during each debate they took part in (see Tables 4.2a and 4.2b for individual candidate performance statistics). Findings suggest near significant differences between candidate tier with second-tier candidates making one joke every three and a half minutes (M=3.59; SD=3.37) compared with front-runners making a humorous comment every five minutes (M=5.25; SD=4.21).[n] This provides a modicum of support for the hypothesis that second-tier candidates will attempt to attain attention through humorous comments more than front-runners.

Analysis of the differences between top- and second-tier candidate humor in terms of target, source of laughter, and length and strength of laughter reveals suggestive patterns. The tier of the candidate making a humorous comment has a near significant influence and is weakly related to whether the target is the in- or out-group as humor by front-runners is more likely to refer to in-group members, whereas second-tier candidates are more likely to focus their barbs on out-groups and competitors.[o] This suggests front-running candidates will want to emphasize their affiliative prowess, whereas the also-rans will want to lower their target's prestige through their attacks.

Likewise, there is a significant and moderately powerful influence of candidate tier on who laughs.[p] Specifically, top-tier candidates are more likely to elicit laughter from the audience and from multiple members of the panel, whereas second-tier candidates are more likely to elicit laughter from individuals, whether fellow candidates or the moderator. Therefore, it appears the status and prestige of front-runners leads to great audience support.

When the length and strength of audience laughter is considered, the judged strength of audience laughter was found not to be influenced by candidate tier.[q] Likewise, there were no significant differences between top- and second-tier candidates in terms of length of audience laughter,[r] nor were differences in audience response found where laughter was followed by applause.[s]

Table 4.2a: Republican Party front-runners and second-tier candidates

	Print Press 5-days prior to debate	Radio-TV 5-days prior to debate	FEC money given 5-days prior to debate	% speaking time during debate
Brownback				
Debate 1	12	28	57,040.20	10%
Debate 2	11	22	44,100.00	11%
Debate 3	5	6	50,960.00	10%
Gilmore				
Debate 1	7	17	12,200.00	10%
Debate 2	10	7	10,150.00	10%
Debate 3	8	11	18,400.00	8%
Giuliani				
Debate 1	85	236	77,4505.00	11%
Debate 2	92	220	630,660.00	10%
Debate 3	81	523	1,290,143.00	16%
Huckabee				
Debate 1	3	48	3,200.00	7%
Debate 2	9	18	10,990.00	10%
Debate 3	6	59	8,055.00	7%
Hunter				
Debate 1	29	16	4,250.00	7%
Debate 2	12	17	6,750.00	6%
Debate 3	20	64	35,835.00	9%
McCain				
Debate 1	60	297	376,492.90	15%
Debate 2	64	148	434,316.00	10%
Debate 3	84	579	412,668.00	16%
Paul				
Debate 1	78	69	43,857.99	7%
Debate 2	97	35	57,046.27	12%
Debate 3	97	31	51,936.00	7%
Romney				
Debate 1	31	438	227,601.80	17%
Debate 2	58	230	548,387.00	13%
Debate 3	96	467	254,948.00	13%
Tancredo				
Debate 1	5	36	15,637.00	9%
Debate 2	4	13	21,843.00	10%
Debate 3	3	15	24,325.00	7%
T. Thompson				
Debate 1	2	107	4,300.00	7%
Debate 2	5	93	23,650.00	8%
Debate 3	5	998	20,485.00	6%

Table 4.2b: Democratic Party front-runners and second-tier candidates

	Print Press 5-days prior to debate	Radio-TV 5-days prior to debate	FEC money given 5-days prior to debate	% speaking time during debate
Biden				
Debate 1	18	10	31,525.00	10%
Debate 2	11	131	203,821.00	10%
Debate 3	6	29	23,317.29	12%
Clinton				
Debate 1	221	474	821,976.00	17%
Debate 2	132	996	1,825,253.00	18%
Debate 3	155	998	1,207,141.00	12%
Dodd				
Debate 1	38	39	37,450.00	9%
Debate 2	20	61	65,650.00	9%
Debate 3	11	71	371,554.81	12%
Edwards				
Debate 1	414	263	183,652.00	14%
Debate 2	376	455	265,531.90	15%
Debate 3	313	998	748,621.99	13%
Gravel				
Debate 1	5	1	00.00	7%
Debate 2	3	6	00.00	4%
Debate 3	4	58%	850.00	10%
Kucinich				
Debate 1	18	86	16,724.54	11%
Debate 2	9	23	10,242.99	9%
Debate 3	15	70	19,278.35	11%
Obama				
Debate 1	111	300	15,741,789.00	18%
Debate 2	89	863	2,435,238.00	19%
Debate 3	87	937	1,830,190.00	15%
Richardson				
Debate 1	25	55	111,450.00	13%
Debate 2	12	152	308,632.02	15%
Debate 3	13	117	404,493.00	13%

Discussion

Findings suggest there are no significant differences between the two parties in terms of whether the focus of humor is on the in-group or out-group, contrary to expectations that Republican candidates would be more likely to focus their comments on the out-group in comparison with Democratic Party candidates. On the other hand, we find that, when comparing use of humor per minute of speaking that the time candidates have during their debates, Republican Party candidates are significantly more likely to make humorous comments at a greater rate than their Democratic Party counterparts. Although this may be seen as reflecting partisan differences in approach to humor, the size of the two parties' slates likely plays a role. Specifically, with the Democratic Party having fewer candidates taking part in each of their debates when compared with the Republican Party, there was likely less competition for media attention (see Table 4.3a & 4.3b) and the need to attain attention through humorous "home run" comments.[30-32]

Support for the assertion that Republican candidates will elicit longer and stronger audience laughter than Democratic Party candidates, is likewise mixed. While laughter length from Republican audiences is slightly longer than that from Democratic Party audiences, and approaches significance, audience laughter followed by applause does not show significant differences between the parties, nor does audience laughter strength. This is likely due to the highly stereotyped nature of laughter,[39, 71] even when group laughter is considered, whereas the signal tends to be sharp and underscores comments without interrupting the speaker. However, while the length and strength of audience response in the form of laughter tends to be uniform across political party, other signaling qualities not coded for might provide insight into partisan differences.[47, 72] For instance, emotional intent can be assessed in laughter from individuals, and even though it has not been evaluated in crowd settings, evaluating the affective nature of laughter might provide further insights into audience response.

Even though few differences between the two parties are apparent, differences between front-runners and second-tier candidates become apparent through statistical analysis. Support, albeit slight, is found for the assertion that second-tier candidates will make more humorous comments than front-runners, likely due to their maximizing attention during the contentious debates through crowd-pleasing comments. Although there is no direct evidentiary link between humorous comments and media attention during presidential primaries, they can prove to be an effective attention-getting tool.[30] The target of the different tiers of candidate is likewise related, with second-tier candidates slightly more likely to focus their attention on the out-group, including direct competitors for the presidency, whereas front-runners will focus their comments on in-group members and themselves, likely underscoring the strength of their relationships in the former, and their willingness and ability to reduce the divide between themselves and their public.

Table 4.3a: Republican Party presidential candidate debate performance

	Number of debates attended	Total humorous comments	Minutes per humorous comment	Mean Laughter Scale (1-5)	Sum Laughter + Applause (seconds)
Brownback	3	1	21.67	2	0
Gilmore	3	1	19.31	1	0
Giuliani	4	8	5.01	2.38	2
Huckabee	5	16	2.70	2.63	22
Hunter	3	4	4.05	1.75	10
McCain	5	21	3.13	2.76	19
Paul	5	4	8.38	2.50	7
Romney	5	11	6.90	2.45	0
Tancredo	3	2	8.89	3.50	6
F. Thompson	1	6	1.98	2.00	0
T. Thompson	3	3	4.83	1.33	0

Tests suggest that while top-tier candidates are more likely to evoke laughter from larger numbers of people, whether the panel or the audience, in comparison with second-tier candidates, who are more likely to evoke laughter from individual candidates and moderators, the length and strength of audience laughter is not significantly influenced. Although this likely reflects the stereotyped nature of laughter, it begs further research concerning the judged qualities of laughter[47, 72] and more precise measurement of laughter onset and offset as well as strength. Finally, as individual laughter might reflect nonverbal communication distinct from humorous intent,[71] the laughter of individual candidates might serve as specific rebuttals to other candidates' attacks. As noted, the great majority of individual laughter, exactly two-thirds, came from front-runners Mitt Romney, Hillary Clinton and John McCain, as they deflected attacks or mitigated comments.

Table 4.3b: Democratic Party presidential candidate debate performance

	Number of debates attended	Total humorous comments	Minutes per humorous comment	Mean Laughter Scale (1-5)	Sum Laughter + Applause (seconds)
Biden	3	3	7.38	3.00	0
Clinton	5	24	3.85	2.25	70
Dodd	3	2	10.73	4.00	0
Edwards	4	3	15.02	1.67	0
Gravel	3	10	1.51	2.67	0
Kucinich	3	1	21.65	3.00	5
Obama	5	22	4.29	2.32	51
Richardson	4	13	3.65	2.69	14

Humorous comment makers

Assessment of candidates on the basis of their individual debate performances provides insight into personal style and audience reaction regardless of whether they are front-runners or second-tier candidates. However, structural attributes of the debates, regardless of party, likely influenced type and amount of humor. Specifically, while both the Republican and Democratic parties had similar sized candidate fields at the beginning of the election, the ebb and flow of the primary season led to the Democratic Party narrowing significantly by the time the Super Tuesday debate occurred, with only Clinton and Obama contending. On the other hand, the Republican field experienced greater transformation, as Fred Thompson entered the field for one debate immediately prior to the New Hampshire primary, and four candidates (Huckabee, McCain, Paul, and Romney) sparred in the fifth and final debate analyzed here, the Super Tuesday debate.

On the Democratic side, it was obvious from the start that Clinton, Edwards and Obama were front-running candidates. Although Biden, Dodd and Richardson presented viable candidacies, they remained mired in second-tier status along with incendiary outsider candidates Gravel and Kucinich. Of the second-tier candidates, Richardson and Gravel made the most humorous comments, both in total and average per minute (see Table 4.3b). Although Richardson has a reputation for being humorous, he did not unleash this humor until his last debate, well after his second-tier status was cemented, making ten of his thirteen humorous comments. At this point his humor appeared more self-deprecatory, and in the instances where he made humorous comments at the expense of his competitors, the tone and content of his humor was conciliatory. On the other hand, Gravel provides an interesting case of a bomb-throwing candidate without electoral hopes whose bombs happened to be highly acerbic quips attacking the other Democratic Party candidates, both individually and as a group, during his three debates. Even then, he provides confirmatory evidence that second-tier candidates will make more humorous comments, and when they do, will attack the out-group, which in this case proved to be the other Democratic Party candidates.

While front-runners Hillary Clinton and Barack Obama made a number of humorous comments, and ranked highly in terms of average humorous comments per minute, the audience response that stands out is that of laughter followed by applause (see Table 4.3b). Here, Obama and Clinton were neck-and-neck, with Obama eliciting laughter followed by applause nine times, and Clinton eight times, followed by Richardson with two events, and Edwards with one event. Clinton far and away elicited the greatest audience response with seventy seconds of laughter-then-applause, trailed by Barack Obama with fifty-one seconds. Both of these candidates can be seen as likely receiving this enhanced response due to the truncated Democratic Party field which saw the two debate each other before Super Tuesday in front of an enthusiastic crowd that laughed at and then applauded humorous comments from Clinton for nearly a minute (fifty-seven seconds) and Obama for just over half a minute (thirty-three seconds). While not as systematic a test as can be hoped for, laughter followed by applause provides a metric of sorts supporting the hypothesis that front-runners will receive greater levels of audience support.

On the Republican side, the candidates able to elicit the most laughter as a per minute average, as well as in terms of intensity, were front-runner John McCain and second-tier candidate Mike Huckabee (see Table 4.3a). Both of these candidates likely saw themselves as underdogs; certainly Huckabee presents a compelling example of an underdog candidate who made his way to attention, if not contender status, through his winning combination of self-deprecatory humor and his witty disparagement of opponents. McCain, for his part, perceived himself as an outsider with most of his humorous comments being acerbic attacks on his competitors, namely Mitt Romney, and the Washington establishment. While Fred Thompson on average was "funnier," with one comment nearly every two minutes, his brief electoral participation in one debate may be seen as distorting the results. On the other hand, his extensive use of humor might reflect a candidate "going all in" to attempt to make a big showing in the New Hampshire primary that followed this debate.

When it came to extended audience response, McCain elicited laughter followed by applause three times, followed by Mike Huckabee with one occurrence. Interestingly, while Ron Paul was able to elicit laughter followed by applause one time during his five debates, Romney was not able to elicit laughter, then applause at all during the five debates. When sum total of laughter followed by applause is considered, Mike Huckabee led Republicans with twenty-two seconds followed by John McCain with nineteen seconds. This suggests that Huckabee and McCain were highly competent in their ability to connect with the debate audiences through their humor, much more so than the other candidates, especially the other front-runners, Rudy Giuliani and Mitt Romney.

Conclusions

Findings here support and build upon evolutionary theory concerning the nature of laughter as a social activity, albeit one with a serious role to play in enforcing group norms and boundaries in the political arena.[37] This is especially the case in more egalitarian societies, such as the United States, where unmitigated aggression to attain status and prestige is not an acceptable approach[24] and where leaders are expected to bridge the divide between them and their followers by reducing their own prestige,[73] even though this self-diminution in prestige may be seen as a form of conspicuous consumption, underscoring the high levels of prestige a leader already has. Specifically, I find that, as can be expected, laughter in competitive situations such as political debates tends to derive mainly from the audience in a show of support for the contending candidates. I also find that the target of the humorous comments aligns with expectations as the majority of these comments are aimed at opponents, whether immediate competitors or an out-group. However, it does not appear that there are differences between the political parties, especially when target of humor is considered, with the possible exception of humorous comments per minute being higher in the Republican camp. Whether this is due to partisan dispositions, individual candidate styles, the sheer number of candidates competing for exposure, thus making memorable moments imperative, or some combination of these factors, party differences in laughter and humor production still require attention.

Analysis of individual candidates suggests that while making humorous comments is part and parcel of a successful candidacy, it is a strategy followed by underdog candidates. Republican candidates John McCain and Mike Huckabee were by a substantial margin the most capable of eliciting audience laughter and applause, and when multiple comments were taken into account, strength of audience laughter. In contrast, while the Democratic Party front-runners Barack Obama and Hillary Clinton are more than capable of eliciting audience laughter and applause, they were superseded by Bill Richardson and maverick candidate Mike Gravel in humorous comments and strength of laughter.

In the absence of presumed front-runners such as seen in the Democratic Party with Clinton and Obama, McCain and Huckabee might have successfully used humor to catapult themselves into public awareness. Specifically, despite his front-runner status, McCain's campaign was seen as moribund and facing financial problems in a face of concerted threats from fellow front-runners Mitt Romney and Rudy Giuliani, whereas Mike Huckabee, an obscure governor from the small state of Arkansas, was seen as yet another face on the dais. Both of these candidates' ability to elicit laughter recapitulates the success of Republican icon Ronald Reagan, the consummate outsider who used humor to puncture opponents, humanize himself and elicit support. Namely, McCain earned himself the Republican presidential nomination, whereas Huckabee received his eponymous Fox news talk show.

Despite the insights provided here, there are also difficulties in studying laughter. Specifically, are candidates successful due to sheer number of humorous comments, or are they successful by virtue of making specific memorable comments that capture the attention of the press and public, often at the expense of other candidates? Humorous comments such as those by Mike Huckabee and Hillary Clinton (discussed at the outset of this article) can have a viral quality, being related by the media long after its utterance. However, a reputation for being funny, with its implications for increased perceived likeability and intelligence of politicians,[1-3] is not built from one joke, but through a series of successful humorous comments that underscores a candidate's connection with the audience.

Notes

[a] Grabe and Bucy[74] (p. 18) argue that Hillary Clinton's tearing up in response to a reporter's query as to the difficulties posed on the campaign trail was responsible for the double digit swing in New Hampshire. While disentangling the effects of humorous comments during the debate from the display of sadness during Clinton's interview is beyond the scope of this study, both incidents highlight the importance of a candidate known for being hard-nosed being able to show vulnerability in public.

[b] Although the study of humor has a long and illustrious history, with the "superiority" theory of humor, in which the purpose of humor is to elevate oneself at the expense of others, attributed to Plato, Aristotle, and Thomas Hobbes, the "relief" theory of humor, in which laughter is seen as the release of excess nervous energy, attributed to Herbert Spencer and Sigmund Freud, and "incongruity" theory, in which the humorousness of a comment is derived from the unexpectedness of the punchline, the lack of a unified coding scheme and the overlapping nature of these theories mitigates against coding on the basis of type of humor.

[c] Research suggests laughter is a form of pre-language vocalization behavior that is "hard-wired" due to it seldom interrupting speech[39] (however, "laugh speak" does occur when individuals laugh and speak at the same time[38]), being automatically induced by others laughing,[36, 45, 46, 75] and being observed as a homologue in mammals such as rats[56, 76] and the majority of primate species.[77] In humans, laughter occurs across cultures, is observed in deaf and blind individuals[50] and interactive vocalizations resembling laughter are evident in infants starting at 5 weeks of age.

[d] The acoustical structure of laughter is seen as occurring in two variants: voiced and unvoiced.[72] Unvoiced laughter occurs in the form of grunts, cackles and snorts. Voiced laughter is "song-like" and is apparent in giggles and chuckles and is more likely to elicit laughter in others due, at least in part, to its being more readily identified. Of the two, voiced laughter is perceived more positively, with laugh-producers seen as sexier and friendlier and more likely to induce the desire to meet the individual, as well as making the rater feel more positive. Furthermore, the emotional qualities can be perceived in different types of individual laughter.[47]

[e] The ability to give nicknames, which are often humorous and derogatory for the owner, can likewise be seen as asserting social dominance by linking individuals to social positions in a humorous manner.[69]

[f] While not coded for specifically, Romney's laughter was distinctly audible during much of the panel laughter during the Republican debates. Whether the strength of a candidate's laughter during a competition for dominance enhances their chances by increasing audience awareness of them (and perhaps being a robust indicator of size), is beyond the scope of this study, but presents future research questions.

[g] While microphones might not accurately reflect the intensity of the audience's response (due mainly to acoustics, but also the physical structure of the event, which might mute response), and hence the intensity of response might be misrepresented here, the perception of those viewing the debates at home are the same as the coders.

[h] $\chi^2(4)=13.690, p=.008, \varphi=.250.$

[i] $\chi^2(1)=.101, p=.751, \varphi=.022.$

[j] Levene test, $F=2.471, p=.121; t(63)=-3.132, p=.003.$

[k] Levene test, $F=1.063, p=.304; t(156)=1.845, p=.067.$

[l] Levene test, $F=3.369, p=.077; t(28)=1.214, p=.234.$

[m] Levene test, $F=3.801, p=.053; t(156)=.665, p=.507.$

[n] Levene test, $F=.295, p=.589; t(63)=-1.755, p=.084.$

[o] $\chi^2(1)=3.238, p=072; \varphi=.122.$

[p] $\chi^2(3)=9.159, p=.027, \varphi=.205.$

[q] Levene test, $F=.001, p=.975; t(156)=-.214, p=.83.$

[r] Levene test, $F=5.062, p=.026; t(102.487)=1.275, p=.205.$

[s] Levene test $F=.016, p=.899; t(28)=.690, p=.496.$

References

1. Bippus, A. Factors predicting the perceived effectiveness of politicians' use of humor during a debate. *Humor: International Journal of Humor Research 20*, 105-121 (2007).
2. Gardner, G., & Gardner, G. Mocking of the president, in *Campaign comedy: political humor from Clinton to Kennedy* (Wayne State University Press, Detroit, 1994).
3. Yarwood, D. L. in *When Congress makes a joke: Congressional humor then and now* 161 (Rowman & Littlefield Publishers, Inc., Lanham, MD, 2004).
4. Priest, R. F. Election jokes: The effects of reference group membership. *Psychol. Rep. 18*, 600-602 (1966).
5. Priest, R. F. & Abrahams, J. Candidate preference and hostile humor in the 1968 elections. *Psychol. Rep. 26*, 779-783 (1970).
6. Baumgartner, J. C., Ed, & Morris, J. S. Ed. in *Laughing matters humor and American politics in the media age* (Routledge, New York; London, 2008).
7. Baym, G. Representation and the Politics of Play: Stephen Colbert's Better Know a District. *Political Communication 24*, 359-376 (2007).
8. Compton, J. More than laughing? Survey of political humor effects research. *Laughing matters: Humor and American politics in the media age*, 39-66 (2007).
9. Feldman, L. & Young, D. G. Late-Night Comedy as a Gateway to Traditional News: An Analysis of Time Trends in News Attention Among Late-Night Comedy Viewers During the 2004 Presidential Primaries. *Political Communication 25*, 401-422 (2008).
10. Fowler, J. H. The Colbert Bump in Campaign Donations: More Truthful than Truthy. *PS: Political Science and Politics 41*, 533-539 (2008).
11. Niven, D., Lichter, S. R. & Amundson, D. The Political Content of Late Night Comedy. *Harvard International Journal of Press/Politics 8*, 118 (2003).
12. Paletz, D. L. Political humor and authority: From support to subversion. *International Political Science Review/Revue internationale de science politique 11*, 483-493 (1990).
13. Pfau, M., Cho, J. & Chong, K. Communication Forms in U.S. Presidential Campaigns: Influences on Candidate Perceptions and the Democratic Process. *Harvard International Journal of Press/Politics 6*, 88 (2001).
14. Young, D. G. The Privileged Role of the Late-Night Joke: Exploring Humor's Role in Disrupting Argument Scrutiny. *Media Psychology 11*, 119-142 (2008).
15. Benoit, W. L. & Hansen, G. J. Presidential Debate Watching, Issue Knowledge, Character Evaluation, and Vote Choice. *Human Communication Research 30*, 121-144 (2004).
16. Benoit, W. L., McKinney, M. S. & Stephenson, M. T. Effects of Watching Primary Debates in the 2000 U.S. Presidential Campaign. *J. Commun. 52*, 316 (2002).

17. Lang, G. E. & Lang, K. Immediate and Delayed Responses to a Carter-Ford Debate: Assessing Public Opinion. *The Public Opinion Quarterly 42*, 322-341 (1978).
18. Munro, G. D. *et al*. Biased Assimilation of Sociopolitical Arguments: Evaluating the 1996 U.S. Presidential Debate. *Basic & Applied Social Psychology 24*, 15-26 (2002).
19. Yawn, M., Ellsworth, K., Beatty, B. & Kahn, K. F. How a presidential primary debate changed attitudes of audience members. *Polit. Behav. 20*, 155-181 (1998).
20. Racine Group. White paper on televised political campaign debates. *Argumentation and Advocacy 38*, 199-218 (2002).
21. Benoit, W. L., Stein, K. A. & Hansen, G. J. Newspaper Coverage of Presidential Debates. *Argumentation & Advocacy 41*, 17-27 (2004).
22. Jamieson, K. H. & Waldman, P. in *The press effect : politicians, journalists, and the stories that shape the political world* 220 (Oxford University Press, Oxford; New York, 2004).
23. Newton, J. S., Masters, R. D., McHugo, G. J. & Sullivan, D. G. Making up our minds: Effects of network coverage on viewer impressions of leaders. *Polity 20*, 226-246 (1987).
24. Dailey, W. O., Hinck, E. A. & Hinck, S. S. Audience Perceptions of Politeness and Advocacy Skills in the 2000 and 2004 Presidential Debates. *Argumentation and Advocacy 41*, 196-210 (2005).
25. Greengross, G. & Miller, G. F. Dissing oneself versus dissing rivals: Effects of status, personality, and sex on the short-term and long-term attractiveness of self-deprecating and other-deprecating humor. *Evolutionary Psychology 6*, 393-408 (2008).
26. Miller, G. in *Spent: sex, evolution, and consumer behavior* (Viking, New York, 2009).
27. Weisfeld, G. E. The adaptive value of humor and laughter. *Ethology & Sociobiology 14*, 141-169 (1993).
28. Weisfeld, G. E. *et al*. Do women seek humorousness in men because it signals intelligence? A cross-cultural test. *Humor–International Journal of Humor Research* (Forthcoming).
29. Zahavi, A. & Zahavi, A. in *The handicap principle: A missing piece of Darwin's puzzle* 286 (Oxford University Press, New York, NY, 1997).
30. Fein, S., Goethals, G. R. & Kugler, M. B. Social Influence on Political Judgments: The Case of Presidential Debates. *Polit. Psychol. 28*, 165-192 (2007).
31. Nabi, R. L., Moyer-Guseé, E. & Byrne, S. All Joking Aside: A Serious Investigation into the Persuasive Effect of Funny Social Issue Messages. *Communication Monographs 74*, 29-54 (2007).
32. Bennett, W. L. in *News, the politics of illusion* 216 (Longman, New York, 1988).
33. Nagourney, A. & Santora, M. Terror Attack Scenario Exposes Deep Differences Among G.O.P. Hopefuls. *New York Times Politics* (2007).

34. Fallows, J. Rhetorical Questions. (Cover story). *Atlantic Monthly (10727825) 302*, 34-52 (2008).
35. Krasner, M. A. *Humor in the 2008 American Presidential Campaign.* Typescript 2008).
36. Hatfield, E., Cacioppo, J. T. & Rapson, R. L. in *Emotional contagion (studies in emotion & social interaction)* 240 (Cambridge University Press, New York, NY, 1994).
37. Alexander, R. Ostracism and Indirect Reciprocity: The Reproductive Significance of Humor. *Ethology and Sociobiology 7* (1986).
38. Chafe, W. in *The importance of not being earnest: the feeling behind laughter and humor* (John Benjamins Publishing Co, 2007).
39. Provine, R. R. Laughter punctuates speech: Linguistic, social and gender contexts of laughter. *Ethology 95*, 291-298 (1993).
40. Attardo, S. in *Linguistic theories of humor* (Mouton de Gruyter, Hawthorne, NY, 1994).
41. Flamson, T. & Barrett, H. C. The encryption theory of humor: A knowledge-based mechanism of honest signaling. *Journal of Evolutionary Psychology 6*, 261-281 (2008).
42. Martin, R. A. in *The psychology of humor: An integrative approach* (Elsevier, Amsterdam, Netherlands, 2007).
43. Provine, R. R. in *The psychology of facial expression.* (ed. Fernández-Dols, J. M.) 158-175 (Cambridge University Press; Editions de la Maison des Sciences de l'Homme, New York, NY; Paris, France, 1997).
44. Kipper, S. & Todt, D. The role of rhythm and pitch in the evaluation of human laughter. *J. Nonverbal Behav. 27*, 255-272 (2003).
45. Provine, R. R. Contagious laughter: Laughter is a sufficient stimulus for laughs and smiles. *Bulletin of the Psychonomic Society 30*, 1-4 (1992).
46. Devereux, P. G. & Ginsburg, G. P. Sociality effects on the production of laughter. *J. Gen. Psychol. 128*, 227-240 (2001).
47. Szameitat, D. P. *et al.* Differentiation of emotions in laughter at the behavioral level. *Emotion 9*, 397-405 (2009).
48. Flamson, T. The encryption theory: Studies in Brazil and the United States testing an evolutionary explanation of humor as an honest signal. University of California, Los Angeles, 1-167 (2010).
49. Platow, M. J. *et al.* "It's not funny if they're laughing": Self-categorization, social influence, and responses to canned laughter. *J. Exp. Soc. Psychol. 41*, 542-550 (2005).
50. Eibl-Eibesfeldt, I. in *Human ethology* 848 (Aldine De Gruyter, New York, 1989).
51. Fridlund, A. J. 5. The new ethology of human facial expressions. *The psychology of facial expression*, 103 (1997).
52. Masters, R. D. in *The nature of politics* 298 (Yale University Press, New Haven, 1989).
53. Salter, F. K. in *Emotions in command: Biology, bureaucracy, and cultural evolution* (Transaction Pub, New Brunswick, NJ, 2007).

54. Marcus, G. E., Neuman, W. R. & MacKuen, M. in *Affective intelligence and political judgment* (University of Chicago Press, Chicago, IL, 2000).
55. Axelrod, R. M. in *The complexity of cooperation: Agent-based models of competition and collaboration* (Princeton University Press, Princeton, NJ, 1997).
56. Panksepp, J. in *Affective neuroscience: the foundations of human and animal emotions* 466 (Oxford University Press, New York, 1998).
57. Janes, L. M. & Olson, J. M. Jeer pressures: The behavioral effects of observing ridicule of others. *Person. Soc. Psychol Bull. 26*, 474-485 (2000).
58. Ford, T. E. & Ferguson, M. A. Social Consequences of Disparagement Humor: A Prejudiced Norm Theory. *Personality & Social Psychology Review (Lawrence Erlbaum Associates) 8*, 79-94 (2004).
59. Spoor, J. R. & Kelly, J. R. The Evolutionary Significance of Affect in Groups: Communication and Group Bonding. *Group Processes & Intergroup Relations 7*, 398-412 (2004).
60. Sy, T., Côté, S. & Saavedra, R. The Contagious Leader: Impact of the Leader's Mood on the Mood of Group Members, Group Affective Tone, and Group Processes. *J. Appl. Psychol. 90*, 295-305 (2005).
61. Hetherington, M. J. & Weiler, J. D. in *Authoritarianism and polarization in American politics* 234 (Cambridge University Press, New York, 2009).
62. Westen, D. in *The political brain: The role of emotion in deciding the fate of the nation* 457 (Public Affairs, New York, NY, 2007).
63. Bono, J. E. & Ilies, R. Charisma, positive emotions and mood contagion. *The Leadership Quarterly 17*, 317-334 (2006).
64. Cherulnik, P. D., Donley, K. A., Wiewel, T. S. R. & Miller, S. R. Charisma Is Contagious: The Effect of Leaders' Charisma on Observers' Affect. *J. Appl. Soc. Psychol. 31*, 2149-2159 (2006).
65. Keltner, D., Young, R. C., Heerey, E. A., Oemig, C. & Monarch, N. D. Teasing in hierarchical and intimate relations. *J. Pers. Soc. Psychol. 75*, 1231-1247 (1998).
66. Keltner, D., Capps, L., Kring, A. M., Young, R. C. & Heerey, E. A. Just teasing: A conceptual analysis and empirical review. *Psychol. Bull. 127*, 229-248 (2001).
67. Chance, M. R. A. Attention Structure as the Basis of Primate Rank Orders. *Man 2*, 503-518 (1967).
68. Mazur, A. in *Biosociology of dominance and deference* (Rowman & Littlefield, Lanham, MD, 2005).
69. Fine, G. A. & de Soucey, M. Joking cultures: Humor themes as social regulation in group life. *Humor: International Journal of Humor Research 18*, 1-22 (2005).
70. Stewart, P. A., Salter, F. K. & Mehu, M. Taking leaders at face value: Ethology and the analysis of televised leader displays. *Politics and the Life Sciences 28*, 48-74 (2009).
71. Provine, R. R. in *Laughter: A scientific investigation* (Penguin Press, New York, NY, 2001).

72. Bachorowski, J. & Owren, M. J. Not all laughs are alike: Voiced but not unvoiced laughter readily elicits positive affect. *Psychological Science 12*, 252 (2001).
73. Boehm, C. in *Hierarchy in the forest: the evolution of egalitarian behavior* 292 (Harvard University Press, Cambridge, MA, 1999).
74. Grabe, M. E. & Bucy, E. P. in *Image bite politics: news and the visual framing of elections* 316-316 (Oxford University Press, Oxford; New York, 2009).
75. Jefferson, G. A technique for inviting laughter and its subsequent acceptance/declination. *Everyday language: Studies in ethnomethodology 79*, 79-96 (1979).
76. Panksepp, J. Neuroevolutionary sources of laughter and social joy: Modeling primal human laughter in laboratory rats. *Behav. Brain Res. 182*, 231-244 (2007).
77. Preuschoft, S. & Van Hooff, J. The social function of 'smile' and 'laughter': Variations across primate species and societies. *Nonverbal communication: Where nature meets culture*, 171–190 (1997).

Chapter 5
Funny Faces:
Presidential Candidate Display Behavior

In the modern televised era of politics, nonverbal communication can impact political preferences and attitudes by bringing the viewer practically face-to-face with the candidates.[1-5] This virtual face-to-face contact leads to a sense of personal interaction though facial displays, bodily postures, and gestures, and vocalic characteristics that influence the viewer's emotional response.[5-8] Thus, politicians who are best able to connect with an audience are more likely to win elections, especially if they are able to inspire positive emotions about themselves while provoking negative feelings towards the opposition.[9, 10]

Humor is just one such tool that may be used to engender positive feelings towards the source through the resultant laughter, often while disparaging the opposition. A candidate capable of eliciting audience laughter through a humorous comment has arguably either established a strong affective connection with the audience or has enhanced a preexisting bond.[11] This connection may strengthen mutual bonds at the same time that it creates distance between the audience and the opponent being targeted, depending on who the target of the humorous comments is.

The use of humor by Presidents and presidential candidates has long been lauded as an effective tool to simultaneously mobilize supporters and alienate the public from competitors. Regardless of their accomplishments, such U.S. Presidents as John F. Kennedy and Ronald Reagan have been highly esteemed, some may say mythologized, due to their personal style. Here, their sense of humor was a key stylistic component with their wit contributing greatly to their public personae and their ability to form a connection with their public. Specifically, these two "charismatic" leaders were able to strengthen the bonds between themselves and their supporters, while gaining followers through their "playful" style of humor, in such a manner that their personal legacy has lasted long after their political careers ended.

That nonverbal presentation can influence whether candidates are perceived as winners or losers has been an intrinsic part of debates[12, 13] since the nationally televised 1960 Nixon-Kennedy debates. Here a youthful and vibrant appearing JFK impressed viewers more when compared to a haggard and tired Richard

Nixon. Furthermore, content analysis of both candidates' behavior suggests that Nixon engaged in behavior out of place for a competitive debate when compared to Kennedy, with higher eye-blink rates and more inappropriate smiling displays.[14]

The importance of nonverbal presentation has remained an important aspect of debate performance, especially with media analyses tending to focus on perceived nonverbal displays of incivility.[15] For instance, President George H.W. Bush was rebuked in the press for looking at his watch during Governor Bill Clinton's response at their town hall debate. Likewise, despite being regarded as the stronger performer in immediate post-debate polls, Vice President Al Gore was taken to task by the media for audibly sighing during his first debate with Governor George W. Bush. This in turn led to public reconsideration of his "win" in that debate.[16] More recently, Senator John McCain was criticized for his impoliteness during the first presidential general election debate of 2008 when he refused to look directly at or respond directly to Senator Barack Obama.[17,a] Perhaps even worse, at the close of the town hall debate between the two candidates, McCain looked lost as he walked in front of moderator Tom Brokaw, blocking Brokaw's summary comments.

Appearing like a leader is often synonymous with appropriate display behavior.[18-24] This in turn is popularly related to asserting control through displaying anger-threat towards competitors.[6, 25] While displaying anger-threat is the most direct and obvious way to assert control, in societies such as the United States that demonstrate egalitarian tendencies there tends to be a distinct preference for leaders who exhibit cooperative behavior with their followers.[26] Happiness-reassurance displays are preferred from our political leaders, so much so that viewers' attitudes toward political leaders may be influenced more by facial displays of happiness-reassurance than party identification, issue agreement or assessment of leadership ability.[7] Therefore, the ability to attack opponents while not appearing rude or impolite, gives a candidate a distinct competitive advantage.[15] Furthermore, the ability to elicit audience support for such attacks through laughter (and applause) signals a candidate's ascendancy by underlining their ability to connect with the audience.[27]

This chapter explores humor and nonverbal display behavior by considering how candidates signal the emotional intent of their humor during the ten primary debates throughout the 2008 American presidential electoral season. I look at laughter-eliciting comments and the co-occurrence of nonverbal facial displays and treat facial displays as signaling the social intent of the humor. Here humorous comments are used in conjunction with facial displays to communicate a candidate's intent, whether to engender affiliative feelings or assert competitive ascendancy, while receiving group support for these actions. In other words, I expect candidates to assert dominance, not just through their successful humorous comments that elicit laughter, but also through their concomitant facial displays of emotions related to dominance.[6, 25, 28] Next, I consider whether specific facial movements and configurations are correlated with audience, as opposed to panelist, laughter as well as whether there is a relationship between different display configurations and the strength of the audience's laughter. Finally, I consider whether there is a relationship between the type of facial display configuration and the target of the humorous comment, whether in-group or out-group, as well as the candidate's political party and the status they hold in the race itself, whether as front-runner or second-tier. Conclusions are then drawn concerning the impact of nonverbal display behavior during debates and how it might affect the election itself.

Nonverbal cues

Humorous comments, standing on their own, often lack context through which they may be interpreted. The dynamic of delivery often establishes whether a comment has humorous intent. As pointed out by Provine[29] (p. 295) "the playful dynamic of the social setting that includes a multitude of nonverbal and postural cues was a more important condition for laughter than a particular verbal message." In other words, how a humorous comment is delivered not only in verbal and vocalic terms, but also in terms of facial and body movement, will affect whether a comment is perceived as humorous, by whom, and the extent of its humorousness. Succinctly, nonverbal cues expressed in the face and body can be expected to affect whether and how loud an audience laughs.

The ability to signal effectively using nonverbal cues in the face and body likely facilitates group cohesion[30] especially as the ability to communicate intentions and motivations clearly assists group regulation.[31, 32] As pointed out by Waller, Cray, and Burrows in their study of the occurrence of facial muscles in cadavers, although there are multiple muscles in the face that do not express equally across individuals and populations,[31, 33] the muscles necessary for the universal facial displays of happiness, sadness, anger, fear, and surprise are all present in human faces and occur with minimal asymmetry. Of these five muscles, only two serve distinctly functional roles beyond communication (the muscle around the eyes and mouth), leading the authors to observe ". . . the nonessential nature of some muscles in producing universal facial expressions may have its basis in the evolutionary development of the facial muscles" (p.437). In other words, the face and its muscles appear to have evolved for the purpose of social signaling.

The extensive research concerning facial displays of emotion have established that not only are these signals universally comprehended, they are also processed automatically,[34] can be picked out from amongst a crowd of faces,[35] and can be identified accurately from distances in excess of thirty meters.[36] Perhaps most pertinently for political candidates, who must communicate not only in the face-to-face intimacy afforded by television coverage, but also must perform to a live audience arrayed at greater distances, in a study by Joseph Hager and Paul Ekman, the facial displays of happiness, surprise, and anger (in males) were accurately signaled with little to no diminished power up to forty-five meters, with predictions for maintenance of accuracy extending to 100 to 220 meters.[36] Furthermore, even in situations whereas subtle facial displays may not be reliably decoded by observers with views that are obstructed or diminished by distance, the highly contagious nature of laughter and/or applause by individuals closer to the candidates may serve to signal group affect.[37,b]

Therefore, nonverbal style of delivery can mitigate the impact of humorous comments, making them less literal, direct, and aggressive and more playful and humorous.[25, 38, 39] On the other hand, innocuous comments may take a harsh turn depending on the delivery of the comment. For example, the same humorous comment made with a smile communicating happiness-reassurance will have a different effect from one made with a "deadpan" or expressionless face, both on the target and the audience.

Table 5.1: Criteria for classifying facial expressions

	Anger-Threat	Fear-Submission	Happiness-Reassurance	Sadness-Appeasement
Eyebrows	Lowered	Lowered and furrowed	Quickly raised	Inner corners raised
Eyelids	Open wide	Upper raised/ lower tigh- tened	Open wide, normal, or slightly closed	Lower raised
Eye orienta- tion	Staring	Averted	Focused, then cut	Averted
Mouth cor- ners	Forward or lowered	Pulled back or normal	Pulled back or raised	Lowered
Teeth show- ing	Lower	Variable or none	Upper or both	Variable or none

From Roger D. Masters, Dennis G. Sullivan, John T. Lanzetta, Gregory J. McHugo, and Basil G. Englis, "Facial Displays and political leadership," Journal of Biological and Social Structures, 1986, 9:330. Modified to include the Sadness-Appeasement category.

Research regarding political figures carried out by the Dartmouth Group[3, 6, 40] and elaborated upon by Salter,[25] focuses on activity in the eyes and mouth and how these reflect emotions and accompanying behavioral intentions (see Table 5.1) in social relationships, suggest that four functional categories of display behavior regulate status and power. Dominant individuals may maintain social order by using anger-threat displays to assert their dominance or may rely on prestige based upon voluntary support from followers.[41] Here, affiliative dis- plays of happiness-reassurance are used to form alliances and support members. On the other hand, responding with either fear-submission or sadness- appeasement displays indicate lower levels of, or reduction in, status. To the extent that competitors for leadership positions exhibit these submissive dis- plays, there will be a concomitant weakening of attributions of status and with it, the likelihood of attaining leadership.[21, 22, 42]

Happiness-reassurance

The facial displays of affiliation are crucial for humans (as well as other social primates) to signal behavioral intentions of affiliation, attachment, and ap- peasement.[43, 44] There are many different types of smiles[45, 46] which can be dis- tinguished by various degrees and shapes of mouth opening,[47] or by the coactivation of the orbicularis occuli, a ring of muscles surrounding the eye and producing cheek raise and crow's feet wrinkles when stimulated.[48] Recent research suggests that different types of smiles have different functions in social interactions,[49] especially as emotion-based smiles regulate cooperative relationships by advertising altruistic intentions.[50-52]

The face serves affiliative functions mainly through relaxed open mouth and silent bared teeth displays. Specifically, the relaxed open mouth display occurs when the lip corners are stretched back and up while the mouth is open and indicates willingness to engage in affiliative behavior, including play.[53-57] The silent bared teeth display, which is also associated with submissive behavior, is used to initiate friendly contact as well as other affiliative behavior and is indicated by the mouth corners being pulled back to show upper and lower teeth in a closed position.[53, 55-57]

It is believed that silent bared teeth displays function as signals of happiness-reassurance behaviors due to individuals living in complex social situations in which the degree status and prestige varies within systems that range from strong hierarchy to egalitarianism.[32, 55, 58] Within these systems, maintenance of relationships are based on individuals' ability to honestly indicate their position in the hierarchy and, as a result, avoid potentially damaging conflicts. In this case, it is important to have explicit signals of power and submission that are distinct from affiliative and cooperative signals. In egalitarian relationships, the need for separate signals indicating power, submission, and affiliation is considerably diminished because payoffs depend heavily on collaborative effort, thus on the strength of the social bond between individuals. This explains why the silent bared teeth and relaxed open mouth smiles are used nearly interchangeably in egalitarian relationships whereas both displays are used separately in hierarchical contexts.[55, 56, 59, c] It also explains why there is a preference for "Happy Warriors," those leaders displaying happiness-reassurance,[7] especially by those individuals living in more egalitarian societies such as the United States.[26, 40, 60]

As noted above, different types of smiles serve different social outcomes. "Felt" smiles, also referred to as emotional or "Duchenne" smiles, are believed to be the spontaneous expression of positive emotion and likely present a homologue of the relaxed open mouth smile. This type of smile is characterized by involvement of both the zygomatic major muscle which pulls the lip corners up and back and by involvement of the obicularis oculi, the muscles surrounding the eyes which are responsible for the opening or closing of these apertures. Research has underscored the social signaling importance of "felt" smiles due to the relative difficulty in voluntarily producing this facial display,[48, 61] meaning it is hard to "fake" and thus is a robust indicator of emotional state and behavioral intent.[d] Specifically, Mehu, Grammer and Dunbar found "felt" smiles increased in sharing contexts,[51] vindicating Brown, Palameta and Moore's suggestion that this type of smile can be an honest marker of altruistic intent and sociable disposition.[50] The implications of identifying social intent in facial displays by politicians was underscored by unpublished findings by Brown and Moore who found that in fifty randomly selected media photographs during the 2000 U.S. presidential race between George W. Bush and Al Gore that Bush was presented as producing significantly more felt smiles, likely leading him to be seen as more trustworthy than Gore.[50]

That individuals would attempt to pose such "felt" smiles to obtain social benefit can be expected, as can the ability for at least some individuals to detect such attempts. These "false" smiles involve the pulling up of lip corners using the zygomatic major muscle involved in "felt" smiles. However, the obicularis oculi, the muscles around the eye aperture, are not engaged,[48, 50-52, 59, 61] so that the appearance of the eyes being slightly closed and/or the presence of "crow's feet" wrinkles on the outside corners of the eyes does not occur. Although "fear" smiles likewise do not activate the muscles surrounding the eyes in the same manner of "felt" smiles, the different appearance of "fear" and "false" smiles suggests different intent, especially as "fear" smiles appear to serve the submissive intent of silent bared teeth smiles, whereas "false" smiles are intended to reproduce the sociable intent of "real" smiles.

The definition of three different types of smiles represents an elaboration on the Dartmouth Group's ethological framework. However, the question remains as to whether these different types of smiles occur in such competitive contexts as political debates and if they do, whether they have an effect on response by competitors and the audience. Furthermore, there is the question as to whether these different types of smiles represent different gradations in strength, or whether they are distinct signals.

Sadness-appeasement

Sadness can be seen as an appeasing behavior that reassures competitors that the individual is incapable of "making a comeback"[62, 63] thus reducing the risk of further attack. This allows the defeated individual to remain in the group and signals the need for social support.[64] In comparison with other display behavior, which often last for only a few seconds to a couple of minutes, sadness usually last for longer periods, running from minutes to hours, even days at times.[45]

Cross-cultural descriptions of sadness indicate down-turned mouth corners, inner eyebrows being raised forming an inverted "U" shaped furrow at the center of the forehead, the eyelids drooping and the skin near the outer corners and beneath is wrinkled, and the nasio-labial fold running from the outer nostrils to the corners of the mouth may be marked.[65, 66] The lack of muscle tonus and the downcast eyes (at times including tear drops) restricts vision, signaling both a high level of appeasement to potential aggressors and need to social supporters.[64]

As a result, displays of sadness tend to be seen as inappropriate for political candidates competing for dominance, leading to a loss of electoral support. Sadness is defined by Ekman and Friesen as a form of distress occurring when one suffers from loss, disappointment, or hopelessness (p. 114). While there are social prohibitions on displaying sadness, especially for men, those who do not show sadness at the appropriate moment, such as the suffering of fellow humans, are seen as non-empathetic. Showing, or not showing, the appropriate emotional display may prove to be a distinct liability in the electoral sphere. For instance, Edmund Muskie, front-runner for the 1972 Democratic Party presidential nomination, who found his campaign derailed when he appeared to cry in response to an attack on his wife.[28] On the other hand, according to Grabe and Bucy, Hillary Clinton's "emotional moment" prior to the 2008 New Hampshire primary in which she displayed sadness, to the point of tearing up, when asked about difficulties on the campaign trail, humanized her and was seen as a key component of her surprise win in the state[23] (p. 18).

Anger-threat

Anger-threat is a relatively unambiguous and readily decoded emotion seen cross-culturally. A major component of the anger-threat display is a fixed stare with brows raised or lowered.[66] These stares become threatening especially as dominant-type individuals stare more than others in competitive situations.[67, 68] The stare, measured by arousal levels, occurs when the eyes are in a horizontal plane. The wide-eyed horizontal stare is most threatening as an element of anger-threat display behavior.[69] The mouth is contracted in anger-threat displays, with the lips either being pressed together when the mouth is shut or "squared" when the mouth is open, showing the teeth.[33, 45] Interestingly, according to Ekman and Friesen (italics theirs) "*(T)he facial signals for anger are ambiguous unless there is some registration of the anger in all three facial areas*" (p. 88). In other words, while the component parts may signal behavioral intent such as interest, the anger-threat facial display configuration is the most effective means of signaling coercive intent.

In addition to (and likely because of) communicating threat, aggressive behaviors attract attention. Dominant individuals are more adept at deploying (or likely to engage in) aggressive tactics as a means of attaining and maintaining attention. This visual dominance, once attained, is attention-getting in its own right.[66, 70, 71] A highly salient example of how symbolic displays of anger-threat might gain attention and establish a candidate as a front runner dates back to the 1980 Republican New Hampshire primary debate when an angry Governor Ronald Reagan, under the threat of having his microphone cut off, asserted "I'm paying for this microphone"—a sound bite that helped boost Reagan's campaign over George H.W. Bush who, during this game-changing moment, appeared disinterested and disengaged.

Furthermore, visual attentiveness signals social power such that the greater the amount of visual attention given, the lower the giver's status compared to that on whom the focus of attention is bestowed.[72] Likewise, experiments find that dominant individuals look more while speaking, but less when listening to lower status individuals.[67, 68] The refusal of John McCain to look at Barack Obama during their first general election debate in 2008 provides an example of how McCain attempted to assert dominance over a less experienced candidate. However, this maneuver had negative repercussions, as McCain was portrayed by the media as being rude.[15]

Fear-submission

Facial display behavior identified with fear-submission across species includes averted gaze, head oriented away from the dominant individual, and closed eyelids.[73] Facial displays of fear-submission in humans have the eyelids in a similar configuration to that of anger, leaving the combination of raised eyebrows and the horizontally stretched mouth as the main characteristics of "fearful" facial displays.[45] The compressed mouth display has been associated with anxiety in interactions with strangers and other unpleasant social interactions.[74-76] Exposure of teeth is variable in stretched-lips display,[77] as some smiles can express appeasement in response to dominant individuals.[57, 66, 78-80] It could be that with both stretched lips and smiles, variability of the underlying mood is associated with the absence of a relaxed mouth, the latter being an important element of affiliative display.

Fear-submission displays often involve the eyebrows being lowered, as in anger-threat displays, albeit with the inner brow raised giving it a furrowed appearance. Additionally, signals of head orientation and gaze provide information, further contrasting fear-submission with anger-threat. Here, the chin is lowered and gaze is averted, as seen cross-culturally with children.[81, 82] This gaze aversion may reduce stress as continuous gaze is disliked, whereas those who avert gaze during conversation are judged to be defensive, evasive, nervous, or lacking in confidence.[83, 84]

It can be expected that in competitive situations such as political debates the affiliative displays of happiness-reassurance will predominate, although agonistic display behavior intended to threaten rivals, such as anger-threat, likewise may be expected to occur, albeit to a lesser extent. This will especially be the case when speakers make humorous comments, as we expect that when affiliative humor is focused on in-group members facial displays will tend to indicate happiness-reassurance. However, when the humor is disparaging and used to attack opponents, display behavior will indicate anger-threat.

Submission and appeasement behavior are not expected to be seen often during debates in which individuals are competing for leadership, as they weaken perceptions of status by their being inappropriately displayed by potential leaders.[18, 19, 21] Fear-submission, when it is perceived in candidates and political leaders reduces prestige.[6] While even more unlikely to be observed during competitive and often contentious political debates, sadness-appeasement likewise leads to reduced status.[42]

Therefore, the types of facial displays that can be expected during debates, specifically in the wake of humorous comments by the candidate and during the audience laughter, will be those associated with dominance. More to the point, happiness-reassurance display behavior will predominate, especially as it is expected there will be a relationship between the display behavior and the occurrence and level of audience laughter.

A key problem to be addressed concerns how the nonverbal cues accompanying humorous comments are communicated and processed. Specifically, signals from the eyes and mouth may be communicated as separate components of the face, or as a configuration of these cues. In the latter case, stereotypical facial displays may be seen as readouts of emotional states (happiness-reassurance, sadness-appeasement, anger-threat, fear-submission). While these expressions may be masked, modified through display rules, or mixed to express more nuanced emotional states,[45] the key starting point is that of reflecting the core emotional state of an individual.

On the other hand, facial movements may reflect the mixed behavioral intent of humor, which is often based upon the social context where it occurs.[46, 85, 86] In other words, due to humor being based upon incongruity, facial display behavior will reflect this incongruity by there not being one specific emotion displayed, but patterns of muscular movement reflecting this incongruity. With this approach, multiple components of a stimulus are appraised, often concurrently, with the resultant facial displays communicating behavioral intent.[87, 88] In other words, the influence of nonverbal behavior might occur through processing of separate components of the face, namely the eyes and the mouth as opposed to specific set configurations.[e]

Therefore, we can expect display behavior associated with the four functional categories will be clustered together. Furthermore, the more display behavior reflects the prototypical dominance display of happiness-reassurance, the more likely audience laughter will occur and the more likely higher levels of audience laughter will be elicited.

The 2008 presidential primary debates

The notation of laughter follows from the previous chapters with candidate, panel and audience laughter being denoted based upon inter-coder agreement. The length of audience laughter likewise follows from the prior chapter, with laughter strength being rated on a five-point scale ranging from "barely audible" to "extremely audible" for increasingly loud laughter, with strong inter-coder reliability.[f]

Next, we considered facial and other nonverbal activity during the "punch-line," the one-to-three seconds after the humorous comment was made and prior to and during the initiation of laughter. Display categories were based upon research carried out by the Dartmouth Group[3, 28, 40] analyzing the effect of facial displays by political figures to obtain and maintain dominance (see Table 5.1). However, unlike the Dartmouth Group and successors[22, 23, 25] which consider facial displays in a holistic manner, display behavior coded here is approached as component units. Specifically, the eyes and the mouth were examined due to their two-to-three seconds of activity providing a high degree of nonverbal information.[89, 90, g]

Facial activity is based upon analysis of the eyes, considering the eyebrows, eyelids and eye orientation, and the mouth (see Table 5.2). Analysis of the eyebrows considers whether they are lowered and furrowed, lowered, normal, or raised. The eyelids were coded on the basis of whether they were open wide, normal, the upper is raised and the lower is tightened, whether they are slightly closed, or whether they are completely closed. With eye orientation, the eyes are coded on the basis of them being either staring, focused then cut, or averted.

The focus on the mouth considers whether the mouth corners are forward, lowered, normal, raised, or pulled back. It also regards how much of the comment maker's teeth show—whether the teeth aren't showing at all, the lower teeth show, the upper teeth show, or both upper and lower teeth show. While the

mouth is the most labile aspect of the face, due to chewing and talking, it is key
for displaying happiness-reassurance when the mouth corners are raised. Further, because we code facial display behavior immediately after a humorous
comment is made, yet prior to and consequent with the onset of audience laughter, we control for potential word production influencing the position of the
mouth.

Table 5.2: Candidate facial displays

Non-verbal cue	Movement	Percent Total
Eyebrows	Lowered & furrowed	11.8 %
(N=187)	Lowered	4.3 %
	Normal	46.5 %
	Raised	31.8 %
Eyelids	Open wide	10.3 %
(N=184)	Normal	53.8 %
	Upper raised/lower tight	0.5 %
	Slightly closed	31.5 %
	Closed	3.8 %
Eye Orientation	Staring	34.2 %
(N=187)	Focused then cut	58.3 %
	Averted	7.5 %
Mouth Corners	Forward	5.3 %
(N=188)	Lowered	0.5 %
	Normal	51.6 %
	Raised	26.6 %
	Pulled back	16.0 %
Teeth Showing	None	28.5 %
(N=186)	Lower	17.7 %
	Upper	36.0 %
	Both	17.7 %

Descriptive analysis of facial display behavior
Nonverbal cues expressed in the eyebrows, eyelids and eye orientation show that
while there is a tendency for the display behavior to indicate happiness-
reassurance, there is enough variance to suggest differentiation in display behavior (see Table 5.2). While raised eyebrows in over a third of the cases are seen
as indicating happiness-reassurance, and the normal position may be seen as a
default of sorts, the nearly 5 percent of lowered eyebrows indicates anger-threat,
whereas the 10 percent of lowered and furrowed eyebrows indicating
fear/submissiveness does raise questions. Although the ethological framework
provided by the Dartmouth Group suggests lowered and furrowed eyebrows
indicate fear-evasion, according to Ekman and Friesen[45] combined with display
behavior in the rest of the face, lowered and furrowed eyebrows might indicate
anger-threat. Therefore, given that 85 percent of display behavior in the eyebrows is either neutral or signaling happiness-reassurance, support the contention that happiness-reassurance displays predominate is found.

That the eyelids remain normal in over half of the coded instances, followed by being slightly closed one-third of the time, and open wide in nearly one-tenth of instances suggests an overwhelming amount of happiness-reassurance display behavior by the speakers, especially as the eyelids were closed just over 5 percent of the time and rarely were seen with the upper eyelid raised and the lower eyelid tight, in a display of fear/submission. This, however, may be due to the ambiguity of the coding of the eyelids as their being open wide may also indicate surprise and anger-threat, in addition to happiness-reassurance. Again, we find happiness-reassurance display behavior predominates.

Finally, with nearly 60 percent of all humorous comments made, eye orientation was focused then cut off, indicating happiness-reassurance. On the other hand, one-third of the time the maker of the humorous comment remained staring, an anger-threat display, while the speaker averted their eyes only 8 percent of the time, possibly signaling submissiveness and appeasement of the target of the humorous comment.

Movement in the lower part of the face, namely with the mouth corners and whether the teeth show, likewise exhibits a tendency towards happiness-reassurance displays, although to a lesser extent than expected from individuals making humorous comments. The mouth corners tend to remain normal over half the time, suggesting a deadpan expression while making humorous comments. In nearly 45 percent of the cases the emotion of happiness or the intent of reassurance may be inferred through the movements in the mouth corners. Specifically, raised mouth corners, as seen in a relaxed open mouth smile, occurred nearly a third of the time, whereas the mouth corners were pulled back 15 percent of the time, as seen in a silent bared teeth smile. In nearly 5 percent of the cases, anger or threat may be seen in the speaker, as the mouth corners are forward just over 4 percent of the time and are lowered very rarely.

Variation in speakers showing teeth was more evenly distributed. Indicators of happiness-reassurance with the upper teeth or both upper and lower teeth showing occurred over half of the time, whereas indicators of anger-threat occurred nearly 18 percent of the time. Finally, nearly 30 percent of the time the speaker's teeth were not observed, suggesting either lack of intent or lack of signaling intent.[h]

In summary, I find extensive support for the assertion that happiness-reassurance displays, indicating affiliative and cooperative intent, predominate. However, by considering only behaviors within functional categories, combinations of facial display behaviors that elicit laughter are not considered. Analysis of how displays cluster and interact likely will provide greater insight into how displays cue laughter.

The question remains concerning whether display behavior, alone or prototypical configurations of dominance, namely happiness-reassurance and anger-threat, and submissive configurations of fear-evasion and sadness-appeasement, influences who laughs and how hard they laugh. Display behavior that corresponds with the Dartmouth Group's definition of happiness-reassurance (mouth corners raised or pulled back, variable showing of teeth, eyelids wide open, normal or slightly closed, eyebrows in variable positions, and eye orientation focused then cut) occurred in nearly one-third of the time (29.7 percent). However, facial displays consistent with anger-threat were rare, occurring in only four of two hundred twenty three cases. Likewise, submissive display behavior of fear-evasion and sadness-appeasement as identified by the Dartmouth Group framework are not apparent.

While prototypical configurations, especially that of happiness-reassurance, can be expected to occur and have an effect on how humorous comments are considered, their definition using the Dartmouth Group's framework is extremely broad. Specifically, it is expected that the closer the display behavior is to the prototype, the more likely it will elicit audience laughter, and the harder that laughter will be when it does. With displays of happiness-reassurance, the starting point is involvement of the mouth, namely whether the lips are stretched back in "fear" smiles, or the corners pulled up as is the case with "false" smiles. The involvement of the eyes in addition to the upraised lip corners in "felt" smiles is expected to add to the power of this display behavior.

The presence of "fear smiles," with the lip corners stretched back occurs, as expected, nearly 15 percent of the time (15.2 percent). Felt smiles in which the lip corners are pulled up and the eyelids are slightly closed occur nearly 20 percent of the time (19.3 percent); on the other hand, "false" smiles which involve only the lip corners being pulled up, occur nearly 10 percent of the time (9.9 percent). Therefore, I find evidence for distinctly different types of smiles occurring during the debates, allowing us to test their co-occurrence with the type and extent of laughter response by panelists and audience members.

Facial display cues exhibited based upon laughter source and strength

Whether laughter derives from the audience, which would appear to be the goal for candidates wishing to develop a stronger relationship with them, or from an individual on the panel or multiple members of the panel, is analyzed next. Here I test the relationship between display behavior and source of the laughter. Findings concerning the prototypical display of happiness-reassurance, as defined by the Dartmouth Group, show no significant relationship between this display and whether the source of laughter is the audience, a candidate, or the panel at large.[i] Therefore, support is found for the assertion that the more display behavior resembles happiness-reassurance the more likely the audience will laugh, is not found.

However, when analysis considering the influence of the three different smiles considers who laughs, I find a significant relationship. Specifically, there is a significant relationship between the display and source of laughter is found.[j] When the different types of smiles are considered, "fear" smiles in which the mouth corners are pulled back, are associated with the audience and, to a lesser extent, the panel being less likely to laugh, whereas individual candidates are more likely to laugh. On the other hand, "felt" and "false" smiles do not appear to be related to who laughs. This suggests that the "fear" smile, while likely socially beneficial by enhancing the likelihood of cooperation, is less a happiness-reassurance display than a submissive display more in line with fear-evasion display behavior. Therefore, the data provides an elaboration on the definition of happiness-reassurance displays.

Figure 5.1: Smile type by source of laughter

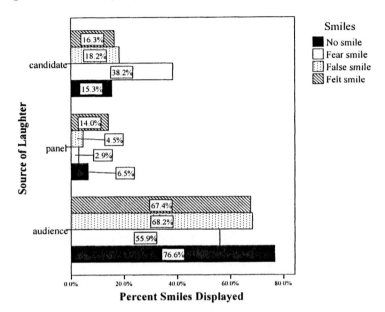

The relationship between display behavior and the level of audience laughter can then be considered, with potential differences in the level of laughter during the debates controlled through an interaction variable composed of debate number by political party. The first equation considers the influence of the Dartmouth Group's happiness-reassurance display on audience laughter. Here I find that, after controlling for the effect of debate itself, the happiness-reassurance configuration is significantly related to the strength of audience laughter.[k] Analysis of the mean scores suggests laughter is louder during happiness-reassurance displays (M=2.80) compared to other display behavior (M=2.27).

When the happiness-reassurance display is decomposed into the three different types of smiles (felt, false and fear), we find a much more attenuated picture. After controlling for the effect of debate itself, the different types of smiles is significantly related to the strength of audience laughter.[l] Consideration of mean scores (see Figure 2) suggests laughter is strongest when the comment maker displays a felt smile (M = 2.97), and weakest when exhibiting a false smile (M = 2.07). Post hoc analysis of the mean scores concerning the strength of audience laughter suggests that, when pairwise comparisons are run, the felt smile is significantly different from non-smiling displays[m] and approaches significant differences from false smiles.[n] Therefore, I find strong support for the contention that the closer the face resembles happiness-reassurance displays the greater the audience laughter strength. Furthermore, findings suggest that false smiles are correlated with lower levels of laughter than all other display behavior, including fear smiles.

Figure 5.2: Smile type by laughter strength

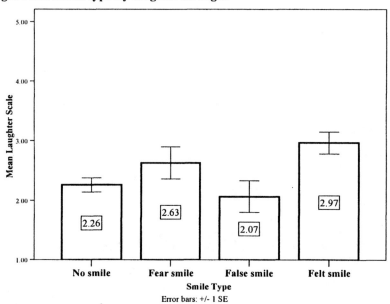

Error bars: +/- 1 SE

Facial displays based upon target, political party and candidate tier

While I have established that facial display behavior is correlated with who laughs and how hard they laugh, the question remains as to whether this display behavior and the target of the humorous comment is related. Additionally, there remains the question as to whether the political party of the candidate making the joke, and the tier the candidate resides in, in other words whether they are a front-runner or a second-tier, also-ran contender, is seen in their facial display behavior. With the target of the humorous comment, it can be expected that there will be a difference based upon whether the comment focuses on the in-group or the out-group, with the happiness-reassurance displays more likely to be associated with the in-group than the out-group, and the lack of display behavior, and even the presence of fear smiles due to their potentially encoding anger-threat, to be associated with comments concerning the out-group. Likewise, facial display behavior and political party the candidate belongs to might be related, especially as the norms and values of the political party relates to how threats to the internal structure as well as external threats are addressed. Here, Republican Party candidates may be expected to display happiness-reassurance to a lesser extent than Democratic Party candidates, due in part to expectations concerning how the two parties approach hierarchy and external threats. Finally, the status of the candidate as front-runner or second-tier will likely have an effect on display behavior as, while all candidates will display happiness-reassurance, especially after comments eliciting laughter, front-runners may be less likely to smile, due to the potential for smiles to indicate submissiveness, and when front-runners do smile, these smiles will more than likely indicate "true" happiness through felt smiles.

Table 5.3: Smile type by target, party and candidate tier

	No Smile	Fear Smile	False Smile	Felt Smile
Comment target				
In-group	56.6 %	13.2 %	11.8 %	18.4 %
Out-group	57.1 %	19.0 %	6.7 %	17.1 %
Political Party				
Republican	59.0 %	18.1 %	8.6 %	14.3 %
Democratic	54.5 %	14.3 %	9.1 %	22.1 %
Candidate tier				
Top Tier	71.2 %	9.6 %	6.8 %	12.3 %
Second Tier	47.7 %	21.1 %	10.1 %	21.1 %
Total	57.1 %	16.5 %	8.8 %	17.6 %

While it may be expected that the target of the humorous comment would be related to whether the candidate making the comment displayed happiness-reassurance or not, and whether the resultant smile was fear, false or felt, no significant relationship was found.[o] Analysis of Table 5.3 corroborates this by showing hardly any differences between the display of felt smiles or no smiles based upon the target with minor differences seen with fear and false smiles, with false smiles slightly more likely to be displayed when making humorous comments about the in-group, and fear smiles when commenting on the out-group.

Likewise, there was a finding of no significant difference in the type of facial display based upon political party of the candidate. Specifically, when a humorous comment was made, it made no difference whether the candidate was a Republican or a Democrat,[p] as norms and values did not play a role in whether the candidate displayed happiness-reassurance and what type of smile was displayed. While inconclusive, when Table 5.3 is considered, the patterns suggest that Republicans, as expected, are more likely to not smile and express the smile most related to the agonic dominance dimension, the fear smile, whereas Democratic candidates are more likely to express felt smiles.

Finally, when the tier of the candidate is considered, whether front-runner or second-tier, facial displays appear to be related. Significant differences in facial display behavior are found with a moderately strong relationship between candidate tier and whether the contender displays happiness-reassurance and the type of smile displayed.[q] Specifically, top-tier candidates are less likely to smile than second-tier candidates after making a humorous comment, with any type of smile occurring less than 30 percent of the time. On the other hand, second-tier candidates display fear and felt smiles just over one-fifth of the time in each instance.

Discussion

The nonverbal cues displayed by the speakers tend to align with the expectation of the affiliative function played by humorous comments that arouse audience laughter, as happiness-reassurance displays predominate. Although there is a good deal of variance in nonverbal facial display behavior with individual indicators of anger-threat in facial displays occurring and making up a substantial proportion of the coded material, the absence of coherent combinations of this display behavior, as well as that of fear-evasion and sadness-appeasement, suggests that intent communicated through facial displays tends to be more affiliative. However, it must be noted that intent communicated through facial displays of happiness-reassurance, as indicated by smiles, has been studied quite extensively in both human and nonhuman primates, with multiple variants identified, including the three used here.

Although this study represents an important step forward by looking at micro-level elements, humor is a complex concept, involving both cognitive and affective incongruity, and needs a more finely honed perspective. Specifically, nonverbal components in facial displays, which were measured categorically in this study, may be considered in graduated levels, as carried out with the Facial Action Coding System (FACS).[45] Here, we can consider whether audience laughter varies with the intensity of either specific facial display components or the strength of different facial configurations or some combination thereof, such as the smiles discussed here. Furthermore, timing can be considered in a more systematic manner. Whereas this study considered the facial displays of candidates in the two-three seconds immediately following the humorous utterance and during the first emanations of laughter, it did not consider whether the nonverbal displays were the product of the humorous comments or the audience laughter that resulted. In other words, while correlation can be ascertained to a degree in this study, causality remains elusive. Future research may benefit by utilizing the cognitive appraisal approach being pioneered by Scherer and colleagues[87, 88] as it may provide even greater insight into the intent of humorous comments and how it correlates with nonverbal cues.

With humor, such as we have seen here, we can expect both core and complex mental states to be encoded in the face, in turn to be decoded by onlookers. Namely, work by Baron-Cohen and colleagues suggest basic emotions are best read in the entire face. Complex mental states are best read in the eyes, whereas the lower face (namely the mouth), does not significantly assist in the decoding of complex mental states.[91, 92] The results presented here appear to agree with these findings as socially relevant information, which may be presumed to have a degree of complexity of intent, appears to be encoded in the eyes of the humorous comment maker both as a separate component and as part of felt smiles.

Furthermore, that the mouth corners play a role in whom laughter is elicited from provides further evidence in support of the power asymmetry hypothesis[55,

[56] distinguishing between two different smiles, the silent bared teeth and relaxed open mouth, with their overlapping, yet divergent behavioral intent.[46, 55] Specifically, humor that arouses laughter from specific individuals on the panel tends to co-occur with the humorous comment maker's mouth corners being pulled back, as seen in silent bared teeth displays that likely indicate attempts at appeasement.[57, 80]

Therefore, it appears that when the audience laughs, there are significant differences in the nonverbal facial displays posed by the candidates making the humorous comments. And as debates are a competitive forum in which candidates vie for public attention and support, it can be expected that the nonverbal facial displays that co-occur with humorous comments will reflect the need to communicate intent, whether it be affiliative or competitive. This finding might be due to the setting in which the humorous comments were made, namely, debates are held in closer proximity to the audience than many campaign events. Specifically, not only does the audience at the event have a better view of the candidates, often being within forty-fifty feet of the speaker as well as large screen televisions, the television audience is placed in proximity to the candidates throughout the telecast. Hence, with campaign events such as these more of the face may be used to communicate intent.

Conclusions

Despite political humor being increasingly studied, and its role in a functioning democracy being appreciated to a greater extent, even when the focus of analysis is on politicians and their use of humor, the greater part of research focuses on the verbal element alone; this chapter addresses the nonverbal element so key in communicating humorous intent and eliciting laughter. Indeed, much of the humor analyzed on the basis of words alone falls flat without the nonverbal cues informing the intended audience as to the intent of humorous comments. Although research by Flamson concerning vocalic qualities suggests humor is not necessarily encoded in voice tone,[93] the evidence presented here suggests that humor, with its emphasis on cognitive incongruity, relies on subtle affective cues predominantly perceived in the eyes, but also in combination with the mouth.

Furthermore, the importance of happiness-reassurance display behavior can be seen with the specific displays of felt, false and fear smiles in particular, in influencing who laughs and how hard. Specifically, fear smiles are associated with laughter deriving from specific individuals on debate panels, suggesting an attempt to appease while diminishing the impact of the humorous comment or potentially suggesting veiled anger-threat displays towards individual opponents. Felt smiles are associated with stronger audience laughter, suggesting there might be an element of emotional contagion deriving from facial feedback. This is especially pertinent as false smiles do not have the same effect, nor are they representations of smile gradations as they are associated with lower levels of laughter when compared with felt and fear smiles and other display behavior.

Meanwhile, the relative absence of submissive behavior, indicating either fear-evasion or sadness-appeasement, can be expected in contests for political support such as presidential debates. That prototypical displays of anger-threat are relatively absent suggests that either they are not encoded during humorous comments or perhaps more globally, this type of display behavior is not considered appropriate for contests in egalitarian contexts, such as U.S. presidential debates. Instead, humorous comments allow for criticisms to be voiced in a civil manner[15] while establishing a positive and strong connection with the audience.

In the modern media age, in which we experience our leaders as if they were present in face-to-face situations, the importance of facial displays for communicating humorous comment intent is accentuated. Laughing matters on the campaign trail, not only by bringing followers together, but in defining leaders. Therefore, the ability of candidates to effectively enhance their status by making a humorous comment relies not only on cognitive mastery of political incongruity, but also the ability to punctuate their comments nonverbally, signaling their emotional state.

As has been shown here, humorous comments made during the primary debates provide defining events for the candidates. Here, they can define themselves by engaging in relational communication that portray them in an informal and friendly manner[13], both in words and nonverbal deed. Even in those cases where humor is used to criticize, the relative absence of anger-threat displays suggests speakers are acting in a polite manner, one befitting a guest of at-home viewers. This intimacy between candidate and viewer, while mediated by television production styles that influence emotional and attitudinal response[5, 23, 94] enhances the importance of understanding visual attributes, including nonverbal cues, in political choice. While much discussion has centered on debates being won not by those who present the strongest substantive arguments, but by those who, according to Lanoue and Schrott[95] best convey "warmth, humor and sincerity on television" (p. 49), these attributes are at least as important in the choice of leaders for a healthy and functional democracy. And while humorous comments may be memorized, the ability to successfully deliver such comments nonverbally does not appear to be so easily coached, potentially making it a robust indicator of candidate character.

Notes

[a] This according to Lanoue and Schrott,[95] interestingly enough, was an area in which Richard Nixon was critiqued during his first debate with John F. Kennedy. Specifically, Kennedy was coached in "what to wear (dark suits), how to sit (legs crossed), and where to look when not speaking (at his opponent)" (p. 12).

[b] This ability to communicate nonverbal cues over great distances was noted by comedian Steve Martin, the first comedian to embark upon headliner status stadium tours of from 20,000-45,000, who in an attempt to enhance his ability to communicate from a distance wore his trademark white suit. Martin notes: "I made quick adjustments for the thundering cheers and the increased audience size. I bore down. My physicality intensified and compressed—smaller gestures had greater meaning—and my comedy become more potent as I settled into deeper into my own body" (p.171).

[c] This is the *power asymmetry hypothesis* which has been observed in a range of social primates by van Hooff and Preuschoft.[55, 56] It is also likely why the Masters and Salter frameworks indicate this display in both fear/submission and happiness-

reassurance categories. Therefore, we expect relaxed open mouth display to indicate greater affiliative intent by candidates,[57] and thus more likely to occur when humorous comments are made. Further, we expect that silent bared teeth displays made during humorous comments will tend to be directed more individually.[49]

    [d] Other indicators of "felt smiles" include the onset and offset time and duration of the smile, as well as its symmetry, with asymmetric smiles being associated with masking behavior, such as in the case of "miserable" smiles that hide negative emotions.

    [e] Research concerning processing of facial display behavior suggests that while the mouth plays an important signaling role, especially when indicating happiness-reassurance,[90, 96] the mouth does not play as significant a role in the identification of core and complex mental states as do the eyes.[89, 90, 92, 96] From birth, social mammals tend to focus their attention on the eyes. The wide-eyed expressions of fear and surprise, in which the schlera (whites) of the eye are accentuated (see Picture 2), is processed precognitively through the amygdala.

    [f] Because audio quality, due to acoustics and recording features, influences the interpretation of the strength of audience laughter, we control for the effect of each venue by including an interaction term for political party (Republican and Democratic Party) by debate (numbers 1-5).

    [g] While the accuracy of Ekman and Friesen's (2003) Facial Action Coding System (FACS) is not disputed, its frame-by-frame analysis is not well suited for dynamic facial activity[90] and is prohibitively time expensive due to 60-90+ frames of activity needing to be coded for each laughter event. Given the accuracy of the approach used here, in terms of inter-coder reliability, and the robustness of the ethological framework, the approach chosen here presents the best investment of time and effort.

    [h] A further step was taken to code for the existence and strength of different types of smiles based upon definitions given in the literature. Specifically, the silent bared teeth smile was constructed by selecting on the basis of the mouth corners being pulled back and the extent of teeth showing. All told, there was a significant subsample of thirty-four cases, with a good quality distribution of whether no or the lower teeth were showing (44.1 percent), the upper teeth only (35.3 percent), or both upper and lower teeth were showing (20.6 percent). On the other hand, the relaxed open mouth smile did now show much range in distribution as in the sixty-seven cases where the mouth corners were pulled up, 90 percent (89.6 percent) involved the upper teeth. The prototypical happiness/affiliation smile, the Duchenne smile, was constructed by selecting for those instances where the eyelids were either normal or slightly closed, eyebrows in a normal pose, eye orientation focused then cut, mouth corners raised, and either upper or both upper and lower teeth are showing. Findings suggest that this pattern occurs in 14.7 percent of the 218 cases in which all facial movements were coded. However, findings for each of these types of smiles did not show significant relationships with the target of the humorous comment and the source/strength of the laughter.

    [i] χ^2 (2, 223) .766, p>.10; φ=.059.

    [j] χ^2 (6, 223) 13.296, p<.05; φ=.244.

    [k] Levene test: $F(18, 139) = .534$, $p=.938$; Effect of debate: $F(9, 147) = 2.447$, $p>.01$; $\eta^2=.130$; happiness-reassurance configuration: $F(2, 14) = 4.457$, $p>.05$; $\eta^2=.030$.

    [l] Levene test: $(F(34, 123) = .926$, $p=.589)$. Effect of debate: $F(9, 145) = 2.691$, $p>.01$; $\eta^2=.143$ happiness-reassurance configuration: $F(3, 145) = 3.420$, $p>.05$; $\eta^2=.066$.

    [m] $t=.025$.

    [n] $t=.076$.

    [o] $\chi2$ (3, 181) 2.302, p=.512; ϕ=.113.

    [p] $\chi2$ (3, 182) 2.096, p=.553; ϕ=.107.

^{q} $\chi2$ (3, 182) 10.186, p>.05; ϕ=.237.

References

1. Friedman, H. S., DiMatteo, M. R. & Mertz, T. I. Nonverbal communication on television news: The facial expressions of broadcasters during coverage of a presidential election campaign. *Person. Soc. Psychol Bull. 6*, 427-435 (1980).
2. Friedman, H. S., Mertz, T. I. & DiMatteo, M. R. Perceived Bias in the Facial Expressions of Television News Broadcasters. *J. Commun. 30*, 103-111 (1980).
3. Masters, R. D. in *The nature of politics* 298 (Yale University Press, New Haven, 1989).
4. Miller, N. L. & Stiles, W. B. Verbal familiarity in American presidential nomination acceptance speeches and inaugural addresses (1920-1981). *Soc. Psychol. Q. 49*, 72-81 (1986).
5. Mutz, D. C. Effects of "in-your-face" television discourse on perceptions of a legitimate opposition. *American Political Science Review 101*, 621-635 (2007).
6. Masters, R. D., Sullivan, D. G., Lanzetta, J. T., McHugo, G. J. & Englis, B. G. The facial displays of leaders: Toward an ethology of human politics. *J. Soc. Biol. Struct. 9*, 319-343 (1986).
7. Sullivan, D. G. & Masters, R. D. 'Happy Warriors': Leaders' Facial Displays, Viewers' Emotions, and Political Support. *Am. J. Polit. Sci. 32*, 345-368 (1988).
8. Patterson, M. L., Churchill, M. E., Burger, G. K. & Powell, J. L. Verbal and nonverbal modality effects on impressions of political candidates: Analysis from the 1984 presidential debates. *Communication Monographs 59*, 231-242 (1992).
9. Brader, T. in *Campaigning for hearts and minds: How emotional appeals in political ads work* (University Of Chicago Press, Chicago, IL, 2006).
10. Marcus, G. E., Neuman, W. R. & MacKuen, M. in *Affective intelligence and political judgment* (University of Chicago Press, Chicago, IL, 2000).
11. Stewart, P. A. The influence of self- and other-deprecatory humor on presidential candidate evaluation during the 2008 election. *Social Science Information 50*, 201-222 (2011).
12. Gentry, W. A. & Duke, M. P. A historical perspective on nonverbal communication in debates: Implications for elections and leadership. *Journal of Leadership Studies 2*, 36-47 (2009).
13. Pfau, M. & Rang, J. G. The impact of relational messages on candidate influence in televised political debates. *Communication Studies 42*, 114-128 (1991).
14. Bucy, E. P. & Ball, J. Quantifying the claim that Nixon looked bad: A visual analysis of the Kennedy-Nixon debates.)Indiana University, Bloomington, IN 2011).

15. Dailey, W. O., Hinck, E. A. & Hinck, S. S. Audience Perceptions of Politeness and Advocacy Skills in the 2000 and 2004 Presidential Debates. *Argumentation and Advocacy 41*, 196-210 (2005).
16. Schrott, P. R. & Lanoue, D. J. Debates Are for Losers. *PS: Political Science and Politics 41*, 513-518 (2008).
17. Cohen, M. A. The first debate: A win for Obama. *The New York Times* (2008).
18. Bucy, E. P. Emotional and Evaluative Consequences of Inappropriate Leader Displays. *Communication Research 27*, 194-226 (2000).
19. Bucy, E. P. & Newhagen, J. E. The emotional appropriateness heuristic: Processing televised presidential reactions to the news. *J. Commun. 49*, 59-79 (1999).
20. Bucy, E. P. Emotion, presidential communication, and traumatic news. *The International Journal of Press/Politics 8*, 76 (2003).
21. Bucy, E. P. & Bradley, S. D. Presidential expressions and viewer emotion: Counterempathic responses to televised leader displays. *Social Science Information 43*, 59 (2004).
22. Bucy, E. P. & Grabe, M. E. "Happy warriors" revisited. *Politics & the Life Sciences 27*, 78-98 (2008).
23. Grabe, M. E. & Bucy, E. P. in *Image bite politics: news and the visual framing of elections* 316 (Oxford University Press, Oxford; New York, 2009).
24. Koppensteiner, M. & Grammer, K. Motion Patterns in Political Speech and their Influence on Personality Ratings. *Journal of Research in Personality 44*, 374-379 (2010).
25. Salter, F. K. in *Emotions in command: Biology, bureaucracy, and cultural evolution* (Transaction Pub, New Brunswick, NJ, 2007).
26. Boehm, C. in *Hierarchy in the forest: the evolution of egalitarian behavior* 292 (Harvard University Press, Cambridge, MA, 1999).
27. Fein, S., Goethals, G. R. & Kugler, M. B. Social Influence on Political Judgments: The Case of Presidential Debates. *Polit. Psychol. 28*, 165-192 (2007).
28. Stewart, P. A., Salter, F. K. & Mehu, M. Taking leaders at face value: Ethology and the analysis of televised leader displays. *Politics and the Life Sciences 28*, 48-74 (2009).
29. Provine, R. R. in *Laughter: A scientific investigation* (Penguin Press, New York, NY, 2001).
30. Dunbar, R. I. M. Co-evolution of neocortex size, group size and language in humans. *Behav. Brain Sci. 16*, 681-735 (1993).
31. Schmidt, K. L. & Cohn, J. F. Human facial expressions as adaptations: Evolutionary questions in facial expression research. *Am. J. Phys. Anthropol.*, 3 (2001).
32. Spoor, J. R. & Kelly, J. R. The Evolutionary Significance of Affect in Groups: Communication and Group Bonding. *Group Processes & Intergroup Relations 7*, 398-412 (2004).

33. Waller, B. M., Cray, J. J. & Burrows, A. M. Selection for universal facial emotion. *Emotion 8*, 435-439 (2008).
34. Stewart, P. A., Waller, B. M. & Schubert, J. N. Presidential speechmaking style: Emotional response to micro-expressions of facial affect. *Motiv. Emotion 33*, 125-135 (2009).
35. Sato, W. & Yoshikawa, S. Detection of emotional facial expressions and anti-expressions. *Visual Cognition 18*, 369-388 (2010).
36. Hager, J. C. & Ekman, P. Long-distance of transmission of facial affect signals* 1. *Ethol. Sociobiol. 1*, 77-82 (1979).
37. Hatfield, E., Cacioppo, J. T. & Rapson, R. L. in *Emotional contagion (studies in emotion & social interaction)* 240 (Cambridge University Press, New York, NY, 1994).
38. Keltner, D., Capps, L., Kring, A. M., Young, R. C. & Heerey, E. A. Just teasing: A conceptual analysis and empirical review. *Psychol. Bull. 127*, 229-248 (2001).
39. Keltner, D., Young, R. C., Heerey, E. A., Oemig, C. & Monarch, N. D. Teasing in hierarchical and intimate relations. *J. Pers. Soc. Psychol. 75*, 1231-1247 (1998).
40. Masters, R. D. & Sullivan, D. G. Nonverbal displays and political leadership in France and the United States. *Polit. Behav. 11*, 123-156 (1989).
41. Henrich, J. & Gil-White, F. J. The evolution of prestige: Freely conferred deference as a mechanism for enhancing the benefits of cultural transmission. *Evolution and Human Behavior 22*, 165-196 (2001).
42. Tiedens, L. Z. Anger and advancement versus sadness and subjugation: The effect of negative emotion expressions on social status conferral. *J. Pers. Soc. Psychol. 80*, 86-94 (2001).
43. van Hooff, J. A. A structural analysis of the social behaviour of a semicaptive group of chimpanzees. *Social communication and movement: Studies of interaction and expression in man and chimpanzee*, 75-162 (1973).
44. de Waal, F. in *Chimpanzee politics: Power and sex among apes* (Johns Hopkins University, Baltimore, MD, 2007).
45. Ekman, P. & Friesen, W. V. in *Unmasking the face* (Malor Books Cambridge, MA, 2003).
46. Fridlund, A. J. in *Human facial expression: An evolutionary view* (Academic Press, San Diego, CA, 1994).
47. Brannigan, C. R. & Humphries, D. A. in *Ethological Studies of Child Behavior* (ed Blurton Jones, N.) 37-64 (Cambridge University Press, Cambridge, UK, 1972).
48. Ekman, P. & Friesen, W. V. Felt, false, and miserable smiles. *J. Nonverbal Behav. 6*, 238-252 (1982).
49. Mehu, M. & Dunbar, R. I. M. Relationship between smiling and laughter in humans (homo sapiens): Testing the power asymmetry hypothesis. *Folia Primatol. 79*, 269-280 (2008).

50. Brown, W. M., Palameta, B. & Moore, C. Are there nonverbal cues to commitment? An exploratory study using the zero-acquaintance video presentation paradigm. *Evolutionary Psychology 1*, 42-69 (2003).
51. Mehu, M., Grammer, K. & Dunbar, R. I. M. Smiles when sharing. *Evolution and Human Behavior 28*, 415-422 (2007).
52. Mehu, M., Little, A. C. & Dunbar, R. I. M. Duchenne smiles and the perception of generosity and sociability in faces. *Journal of Evolutionary Psychology 5*, 183-196 (2007).
53. de Marco, A., Petit, O. & Visalberghi, E. The Repertoire and Social Function of Facial Displays in Cebus capucinus. *Int. J. Primatol. 29*, 469-486 (2008).
54. Visalberghi, E., Valenzano, D. R. & Preuschoft, S. Facial displays in Cebus apella. *Int. J. Primatol. 27*, 1689-1707 (2006).
55. Preuschoft, S. & Van Hooff, J. The social function of "smile" and "laughter": Variations across primate species and societies. *Nonverbal communication: Where nature meets culture*, 171–190 (1997).
56. van Hooff J.A.R.A.M., P. S. Laughter and smiling: the intertwining of nature and culture. *Animal Social Complexity*, 260-287 (2003).
57. Waller, B. M. & Dunbar, R. I. M. Differential behavioural effects of silent bared teeth display and relaxed open mouth display in chimpanzees (Pan troglodytes). *Ethology 111*, 129-142 (2005).
58. Parr, L. A., Waller, B. M. & Fugate, J. Emotional communication in primates: implications for neurobiology. *Curr. Opin. Neurobiol. 15*, 716-720 (2005).
59. Mehu, M. & Dunbar, R. I. M. Naturalistic observations of smiling and laughter in human group interactions. *Behaviour 145*, 1747-1780 (2008).
60. Warnecke, A. M., Masters, R. D. & Kempter, G. The roots of nationalism: Nonverbal behavior and xenophobia. *Ethol. Sociobiol. 13*, 267-282 (1992).
61. Ekman, P. Behavioral markers and recognizability of the smile of enjoyment. *Journal of Personality and Social Psychology 64*, 83-93 (1993).
62. Sloman, L. & Price, J. S. Losing behavior (yielding subroutine) and human depression: Proximate and selective mechanisms. *Ethol. Sociobiol. 8*, 99-109 (1987).
63. Gardner Jr, R. Mechanisms in manic-depressive disorder: An evolutionary model. *Arch. Gen. Psychiatry 39*, 1436-1441 (1982).
64. Hasson, O. Emotional Tears as Biological Signals. *Evolutionary Psychology 7*, 363-370 (2009).
65. Darwin, C., Ekman, P. & Prodger, P. in *The expression of the emotions in man and animals* (Oxford University Press, New York, NY, 2002).
66. Eibl-Eibesfeldt, I. in *Human ethology* 848-848 (Aldine De Gruyter, New York, 1989).
67. Exline, R. V., Ellyson, S. L. & Long, B. Visual behavior as an aspect of power role relationships. *Nonverbal communication of aggression 2*, 21–51 (1975).

68. Dovidio, J. F. & Ellyson, S. L. Patterns of visual dominance behavior in humans. *Power, dominance, and nonverbal behavior*, 129–149 (1985).
69. Morris, D. in *The naked ape: a zoologist's study of the human animal* (Cape, 1967).
70. Chance, M. R. A. Attention Structure as the Basis of Primate Rank Orders. *Man 2*, 503-518 (1967).
71. Mazur, A. in *Biosociology of dominance and deference* (Rowman & Littlefield, Lanham, MD, 2005).
72. Hold-Cavell, B. C. L. Showing-off and aggression in young children. *Aggressive Behav. 11*, 303-314 (2006).
73. Marler, P. Communication in monkeys and apes. *Primate behavior*, 544–584 (1965).
74. Grant, E. C. Human facial expression. *Man 4*, 525-692 (1969).
75. Givens, D. Greeting a stranger: Some commonly used nonverbal signals of aversiveness. *Semiotica 22*, 351-368 (1978).
76. Smith, W. J., Chase, J. & Lieblich, A. K. Tongue showing: a facial display of humans and other primate species. *Semiotica 11*, 201-246 (1974).
77. Seaford, H. W. J. Maximizing replicability in describing facial behavior. *Semiotica 24*, 1-32 (1978).
78. Ekman, P., Friesen, W. V. & Ancoli, S. Facial signs of emotional experience. *J. Pers. Soc. Psychol. 39*, 1125-1134 (1980).
79. Ekman, P. Smiles when lying. *J. Pers. Soc. Psychol. 54*, 414-420 (1988).
80. Dunbar, R. I. M. Relationship between Smiling and Laughter in Humans (Homo sapiens): Testing the Power Asymmetry Hypothesis. *Folia Primatol. 79*, 269-280 (2008).
81. McGrew, W. Aspects of social development in nursery school children, with emphasis on introduction to the group. *Ethological studies of child behaviour*, 129–156 (1972).
82. Stern, D. N. & Bender, E. P. *An ethological study of children approaching a strange adult: Sex differences* (Sex differences in behavior: a conference, Krieger Pub Co, 1974).
83. Kleinke, C. L. Gaze and eye contact: A research review. *Psychol. Bull. 100*, 78-100 (1986).
84. Kraut, R. E. & Poe, D. B. Behavioral roots of person perception: The deception judgments of customs inspectors and laymen. *J. Pers. Soc. Psychol. 39*, 784-798 (1980).
85. Fridlund, A. J. 5. The new ethology of human facial expressions. *The psychology of facial expression*, 103 (1997).
86. Russell, J. A., Bachorowski, J. & Fernandez-Dols, J. Facial and vocal expressions of emotion. *Annu. Rev. Psychol.*, 329-350 (2003).
87. Scherer, K. R., Schorr, A. & Johnstone, T. in *Appraisal processes in emotion: Theory, methods, research* (Oxford University Press, USA, 2001).
88. Scherer, K. R. & Ellgring, H. Are facial expressions of emotion produced by categorical affect programs or dynamically driven by appraisal. *Emotion 7*, 113-130 (2007).

89. Ambadar, Z. Deciphering the enigmatic face: The importance of facial dynamics in interpreting subtle facial expressions. *Psychological Science 16*, 403-410 (2005).
90. Nusseck, M., Cunningham, D. W., Wallraven, C. & Bülthoff, H. H. The contribution of different facial regions to the recognition of conversational expressions. *Journal of Vision 8*, 1-23 (2008).
91. Baron-Cohen, S. & Wheelwright, S. The 'Reading the Mind in the Eyes' Test Revised Version: A Study with Normal Adults, and Adults with Asperger Syndrome or High-functioning Autism. *Journal of Child Psychology & Psychiatry & Allied Disciplines 42*, 241-251 (2001).
92. Baron-Cohen, S., Wheelwright, S. & Jolliffe, T. Is There a "Language of the Eyes"? Evidence from Normal Adults, and Adults with Autism or Asperger Syndrome. *Visual Cognition 4*, 311-331 (1997).
93. Flamson, T. The encryption theory: Studies in Brazil and the United States testing an evolutionary explanation of humor as an honest signal. University of California, Las Angeles, CA 1-167 (2010).
94. Wicks, R. H. Does Presentation Style of Presidential Debates Influence Young Voters' Perceptions of Candidates? *Am. Behav. Sci. 50*, 1247-1254 (2007).
95. Lanoue, D. J. & Schrott, P. R. in *The Joint Press Conference: The history, impact, and prospects of American presidential debates* 173 (Greenwood Press, Westport, CT, 1991).
96. Smith, M. L., Cottrell, G. W., Gosselin, F. A. & Schyns, P. G. Transmitting and decoding facial expressions. *Psychological Science 16*, 184 (2005).

Chapter 6
"Likeable Enough":
Hillary Clinton, Mike Huckabee, John McCain, and Barack Obama

When seen from a broad perspective, analysis of the use of humor during primary debates provides insights into the patterns of humorous comment targets and nonverbal delivery as well as audience response. While this information undoubtedly is useful for understanding campaign humor as a whole, it is the individual that makes the humorous comments and runs the risks of a failed attempt at humor or reaps the rewards of audience laughter. Understanding the content of humorous comments and delivery by individual candidates provides insight into not just the candidate him or herself, but also provides a window through which audience support for these presidential candidates may be viewed and understood. Specifically, the humorous utterances by the candidates and their nonverbal delivery style, as seen in the face, provides a "thin slice" perspective by which candidates intelligence, personality and the social-political norms they support may be judged. Appreciating this is especially important when observing the rise and fall of candidates with some solidifying their position as presidential front-runners, while others vault into the top-tier on the basis of their ability to elicit audience laughter.

As we have seen throughout this book, humor is an extremely difficult concept to define. By using John Morreall's basic pattern for humor, which states that there is a rapid cognitive shift in thoughts and/or perceptions, an engagement in a "play" mode disengaged from concerns, and that there is enjoyment of this cognitive shift signaled through laughter,[1] I have worked backwards from the laughter to the signaling of the "play" through facial displays (or their absence) while considering the target.

The focus of this chapter is on the cognitive component, as posited by Morreall's humor pattern; in other words, the spotlight will be on the utterances themselves. The humorous comments can be expected to reveal information about not just the audience's connection with the candidate (as signaled by laughter), but also about the candidate's norms and values and the personality traits they possess. Our analysis utilizes Flamson and Barrett's "encryption theory of humor"[2, 3] which points out that "humor functions as an honest signal of the fact of common knowledge, attitudes, and preferences" (p. 262) to understand the dynamic relationship between the audience and candidate. According to this approach, humor is "funnier" when it signals background knowledge and values not completely known and appreciated by all listeners, but only a privileged few "in the know" and/or having shared values, personality, and experiences. This in turn does much to signal in-group belonging[4, 5, 6] while potentially ostracizing those who do not belong to the group.[5]

At the same time, humorous comments signal qualities possessed by its maker such as intelligence and personality traits.[7, 8] While a modicum of intelligence can be seen as valued across all candidates for leadership positions, certain personality traits are valued more in leaders, with variation in preference for these qualities expected to occur across the political parties. For instance, Kevin Smith et al.[9] found leaders who were seen as not craving positions of power, yet who had earned them were valued, even beloved, especially by those individuals who were more trusting and generous.[a] Thus, candidates who successfully attack their opponents' motives, often through suggesting the willingness of their opponents to do anything to get elected, including changing positions on a regular basis, are more likely to successfully impugn their opponent. This is especially the case when humor is used, as more aggressive attacks may backfire due to being deemed "impolite."[10] Likewise, as discussed extensively in chapter 2, self-deprecatory humor may be used to signal the relative lack of political ambition, or at the very least, to mitigate the extremity of perceived concerns.

Furthermore, some personality traits seem to be favored more by the different political parties. The focus on preserving in-group boundaries and moral values within the Republican Party, in comparison with the focus on conscientiousness and agreeableness within Democratic Party identifiers, will likely be seen in the humor preferred by that party's candidates. Although these candidates may try to appropriate the issues[11] and personality traits associated with the opposing party during the general election, the focus will likely be upon reflecting the core political values of the primary voters.

To allow for a more complete understanding of humor, this chapter will focus on the four candidates who appeared to benefit most by their use of humor, with two from each political party. Specifically, I focus on the two most humorous candidates on the Republican side, John McCain and Mike Huckabee. McCain's acerbic wit is a well-known commodity, and one put to good use during his campaign to win his party's nomination. Mike Huckabee not only catapulted himself from a nearly unknown candidate to a strong challenger, but has also been able to establish himself as a continuing voice in the political conversation due in large part to his sense of humor. On the Democratic side we consider Hillary Clinton and Barack Obama. While neither candidate was seen as particularly funny in the early stages of the campaign, both were able to burnish their profile due in part to their ability to connect with their audiences through humor later in their primary campaigns.

The means used to understand the humor of these four candidates includes analysis of the humorous utterances themselves in terms of who the target was, whether it appeared to be prepared material or spontaneous, and what the results of the specific comments were in terms of media coverage. In addition, how the humorous comments are delivered is considered by analyzing the facial displays of the candidates, as is the manner in which the candidates responded to humor focused on them. This information is then digested and considered in light of what they say about the personality of the presidential candidates as well as the social and political norms held by them. While the analysis presented here is expected to provide insights into the public personae of the four candidates, and by extrapolation, that of their personalities, it should be noted that this chapter is exploratory in nature, with inferences drawn being incomplete and hopefully leading to future research.

Hillary Clinton

During Hillary Clinton's first three debates, she did not generate much in terms of humor. This was likely due to both the multi-candidate debate format that inhibited comfortable give-and-take for the use of humor to jockey for attention as well as Clinton's awareness of her front-runner status that could be tarnished by an untimely or misplayed humorous comment. When Clinton did make humorous comments in these early debates, they were either unintentionally humorous, as with her comments about Joe Biden which inadvertently made light of his age, and from which she quickly backpedaled, or they were self-deprecatory. In this latter case, she made a pre-emptive jibe about her being compared to Paris Hilton, apparently in reference to comments about Obama's celebrity status. In each of these events, Clinton showcased a level of quick-wittedness.

The one case in the early debates in which Hillary Clinton went on the attack using humor that was apparently prepared was in reference to the Bush Administration's foreign policy. Here she made fun of the Administration generally and Dick Cheney specifically, saying: "They have, every so often, Condi Rice go around the world and show up somewhere and make a speech and occasionally they even send Dick Cheney, that's hardly diplomatic in my view." This line, however, did not resonate beyond the confines of the audience, in spite of eliciting strong laughter.

However, Hillary Clinton experienced a game-changing moment during the New Hampshire debate when she responded to a moderator question about her "likeability." Here she was asked about New Hampshire poll findings that showed she was respected although not liked as much in comparison with Obama. Clinton affected anguish, stating "Well …that hurts my feelings," smiling and sighing in resignation. She then melodramatically responded, "But I'll try to go on," before she noted "I don't think I'm that bad." Here, with her self-deprecatory wit Clinton not only signaled her quick intellect and her willingness to diminish her status as a front-runner and high-status politician vis-à-vis the audience, but also her ability to "play" with the audience. Specifically, she was able to elicit audience laughter four times in quick succession.

Newspaper coverage of the New Hampshire debate's aftermath suggested that not only did Clinton enhance her likeability, she also made herself appear more approachable and compassionate. Furthermore, Clinton's self-deprecatory humor and Obama's perceived non-playful non-verbal non-response created a wedge of apparent sexism in the women interviewed in the wake of the debates.[b] This drove down support for Obama as the voters interviewed afterward found his response, "condescending, and an echo of other unkind remarks about women over the years."[12]

Whether or not Obama's remark was intended as patronizing, or was just a matter of his being focused on preparing for the next question, a wedge was inserted into the electorate. As a result, Obama was portrayed as less likeable than a newly approachable Hillary Clinton, who became even more humanized with her display of vulnerability a few days later when she nearly teared up when confessing the difficulties experienced on the campaign trail.[13] The resulting upwelling of support for Clinton, and concurrent ebbing of support for Obama, led to a surprise New Hampshire victory for Clinton, and underscores the game-changing nature of self-deprecatory and humanizing humor.

While the New Hampshire debate proved to be a defining moment in the use of humor by Hillary Clinton, it also appeared to lead to her to unleash her wit in the Super Tuesday debate with Barack Obama. Here, she not only responded with spontaneous humor to questions and attacks by the moderators, she also utilized what appeared to be prepared humorous comments to attack the Bush Administration. Specifically, she made six comments ridiculing the Republican administration's handling of the economy and foreign policy, making comments concerning how "you know it did take a Clinton to clean after the first Bush and I think it might take another one to clean up after the second Bush" to audience laughter followed by applause.

When Clinton made quips focused on Obama, they were genial, almost collegial as she made comments such as, "Well, I have to agree with everything Barack just said." Clinton's comments seemed to reach across the divide between Obama's supporters and herself as she appeared to woo them by requesting them to visit her website, saying, "I want your folks to participate too." In all, her humorous exchanges with her competitors were highly amiable, especially in the debate immediately prior to Super Tuesday.

Interestingly, the sharpest exchange involving Clinton in which audience laughter was elicited was a salvo exchanged between Clinton and moderator Wolf Blitzer. Here, Clinton attempted to laugh off Blitzer's pointed comments concerning her support of the Iraq War. When Blitzer attempted to get her on a "gotcha" question, the audience started booing Blitzer in support of Clinton, laughing with her when she jousted with Blitzer, saying "well, let me, you asked the question of me, I, you know I deserve to answer" followed by "I think that, you know that is a good try Wolf."

The nonverbal behavior of Hillary Clinton—"The Clinton Cackle"

Not since Howard Dean unleashed his infamous "Dean scream" in 2004[13] has a presidential primary candidate come under such scrutiny for a nonverbal utterance as Hillary Clinton came for her laughter. This laughter was dubbed the "Clinton Cackle" by critics on both the left and right who framed her laughter as being similar to a hen's or a witch's cackle. Rightly or wrongly, questions concerning the authenticity of her laughter surfaced early in the campaign when Clinton laughed off pointed questions from interviewers such as CBS News' Bob Schieffer, Fox News' Chris Wallace, and HBO's Bill Maher.[14, 15] While much has been made of her laughter, with associated conjecture concerning the intent and spontaneity of it, no systematic analysis has been carried out. The data considered here, while incomplete in coverage of the campaign, with only ten debates, and non-inclusive of an individual candidate's laughter that infects other candidates and the audience, provides a basis for understanding what induced Clinton's laughter in terms of who made the utterance, what the comment addressed, and who the target was during these debates.

While Clinton's solo laughter is certainly apparent numerous times throughout the course of the five debates in which she took part in, she was not alone in this regard. Her fifteen solo laughter events match well with John McCain's fourteen laughter events and were dwarfed in comparison by Mitt Romney's twenty-one solo laughter events. The substance of the laughter eliciting comments, however, tells a more nuanced story. Three-quarters of the solo laughs by Clinton came as a result of interactions with the debate moderators. While a few of her laughter events were in response to innocuous questions and comments by CNN's Wolf Blitzer, Politico's Jeanne Cummings, Doyle Mac-Manus of the Los Angeles Times, and New Hampshire television station WMUR's Scott Spradling, others appeared to serve to deflect attacks. Specifically, Clinton laughed when, during the second debate, Blitzer asked her about her thoughts concerning Barack Obama's health care plan, prefacing his question by stating "So Senator Clinton, you've been involved in this issue, as all of us remember, for a long time."

Clinton likewise laughed when asked to second-guess Bill Clinton when Blitzer asked "So Senator Clinton, the question was, was your husband's decision to all this don't ask don't tell policy to go forward. He was president of the United States, he could have changed it, uh, was it a mistake?"

Although Blitzer elicited nearly half of Clinton's solo laughs, perhaps the most straightforwardly aggressive questions came from Politico's Jeanne Cummings. Two questions posed by Cummings focused on the candidate's pedigree as a Clinton where the correspondent first asked about her capability to affect Washington, DC, politics, querying "How can you be an agent of change when we have had the same two families in the White House for the last thirty years?" Cummings later followed up with a more sharply worded question concerning Bill Clinton's tendency to "go rogue" asking, "If your campaign can't control your (husband), the former President now, what will it be like when you're in the White House?"[c]

Despite being a consistent front-runner and the early leader, Clinton only sustained attacks from fellow candidates that elicited her solo laughter three times. In her second debate Clinton laughed off a veiled attack by John Edwards concerning her vote on funding the Iraq War and that, furthermore, she was not leading but instead was legislating. Likewise, she laughed when, after having her position on invading Iraq attacked by both candidates Barack Obama and John Edwards during the New Hampshire debate, moderator Scott Spradling pointed this apparent double-team effort out, with Clinton commenting, "I'm glad you noticed." The pointing out of both Edwards and Obama confronting Clinton's position may have set the stage for Clinton's game-changing self-deprecatory comments discussed earlier that may have helped her win the New Hampshire primary, especially as her self-deprecatory comments occurred only moments later. Specifically, the actions of both candidates and the moderator's recognition of their attacks on her position allowed Clinton to punctuate her victimized status with a laugh before she demurred to not being as likable as Obama.

Table 6.1: The "Big Four's" facial display behavior

	Felt Smile	False Smile	Fear Smile	No Smile
Clinton (N=26[2])	25.0%	16.6%	25.0%	33.3%
Huckabee (N=23[4])	0.0%	0.0%	5.3%	94.7%
McCain (N=36[6])	26.6%	0.0%	33.3%	40.0%
Obama (N=27[5])	18.2%	0.0%	4.5%	77.3%

While Hillary Clinton's laughter received the greatest amount of press attention, her facial displays after making humorous comments showed the greatest variance of all four candidates considered, with her display behavior being distributed amongst felt, false and fear smiles, as well as "no smile." Furthermore, she was least likely to remain deadpan and the only candidate of the four (Clinton, Huckabee, McCain and Obama) to display false smiles. Here, Clinton's facial response involved only her mouth corners raising without her eyes being involved, and occurred chiefly in response to attacks on her. Perhaps most telling is that her "likeability" moment during the New Hampshire debate was punctuated by felt smiles involving both the mouth corners being raised and her eye corners being slightly closed. This suggests that the moment with the greatest resonance occurred when Clinton was most obviously enjoying herself.

Barack Obama

In spite of his being defined by the press as a serious-minded candidate not much given to humor, Barack Obama generated his share of audience laughter. However, as was seen with Hillary Clinton, Obama's humor only became readily apparent during the relaxed, almost amiable, Super Tuesday debate. During the first three debates the audience laughter elicited by Obama tended to stem from his quick witted response to other candidates. Specifically, when outsider Mike Gravel attacked him and the other mainstream candidates nuclear weapons' policy, Obama responded by stating "I'm not planning to nuke anybody right now Mike, I promise you" drawing audience laughter. And when Joe Biden made a non sequitur statement about AIDS testing that led audiences to infer Biden stated he and Obama were a couple, Obama responded "Tavis, Tavis, I, I, just to make clear, I got tested with Michelle (Obama)." Finally, when asked about how he would utilize ex-President Bill Clinton, he qualified his comments by stating "Now obviously Senator Clinton may have something to say about how I use, ah, Bill Clinton." In sum, his humor in these early debates was polite and deflected any attacks or misrepresentations that may have been made through a ready wit. Furthermore, it seems to underscore the need to treat female candidates with greater politeness and respect than male candidates, as Obama used the more familiar first names for the males he responded to. However, when Obama made reference to Hillary Clinton, he accorded her greater deference, referring to her by the honorific "Senator Clinton."[d]

The one case in which Obama appeared to use prepared humor that seemed to have encrypted elements occurred during the third debate on PBS with Tavis Smiley hosting. Here, he took the Bush Administration to task for their handling of the aftermath of Hurricane Katrina, and their apparent tone-deaf response to the needs of the less affluent members of society. Specifically, he mocked the Bush Administration by commenting "Because part of the reason that we had such a tragedy was the assumption that everybody could jump in their SUVs, load up with some sparkling water, and check into the nearest hotel." This comment subtly primed the economic divide between "haves" and "have-nots" by referring to such loaded terms as "SUVs" and "sparkling water." Furthermore, SUV, due to its environmental implications, primes certain responses for a key demographic of the Democratic Party. While this humor certainly resonated with the audience, it was also a safe choice for humor, given the "home field advantage" he enjoyed with an audience composed mainly of blacks who felt the neglect of the Bush Administration, most especially during Hurricane Katrina.

The New Hampshire debate provided Obama with the opportunity to take a dig at the Republican Party candidates, who took part in their debate earlier that evening in the same room, while burnishing his credentials as a football fan, already well established during his campaign. Here, he admitted "that I was going back and forth between the Republicans and football," playing upon the typical football fan's need to keep up with his or her team while getting a dig into the non-essential nature of the Republican debates, which did not demand full attention. While this comment certainly resonated with the audience and, presumably, football fans, especially those of the Redskins, the debate became remembered for his response, or lack thereof, to Hillary Clinton's masterful use of self-deprecatory humor discussed earlier.

However, it was during the Super Tuesday debate that Barack Obama's humor became most evident, as he made several witticisms, self-deprecatory comments and humorous attacks ridiculing the Republican Party's policies. In this latter case, Obama's remarks focused on economic matters as he made what appeared to be several prepared humorous comments. In response to the Republican Party candidates' economic policies as a group, he stated, "Well first of all, uh, I don't think the Republicans are going to be in a real strong position to argue fiscal responsibility (laughter) when they've added four, five trillion dollars worth of national debt."

He also focused his comments on individual candidates. Taking Republican candidate and businessman Mitt Romney to task about his fiscal abilities, Obama commented "let me just also point out that a Mitt Romney hasn't gotten a very good return on his investment during this presidential campaign." He further twisted the jibe, saying "I'm happy to take a look at my management style during the course of this last year and his . . ." and "I think they compare fairly well." Front-runner John McCain was not exempt from his jibes, as Obama stated in reference to McCain's shifting his position on tax cuts from fiscal responsibility to supporting them, even during wartime, that "And somewhere along the line the Straight Talk Express lost some wheels," a line that was recycled during the general election debates, albeit with diminished success.

While he did take a swipe at fellow Democratic Party candidate Hillary Clinton's position on entering into the Iraq conflict stating, "Now, you, at this point, she's got a clear position, but it took a while," drawing a laugh from Clinton herself as she shrugged off the comment, most of his comments concerning Clinton were conciliatory in tone. In responding to Wolf Blitzer's question "Would you consider an Obama-Clinton or Clinton-Obama ticket going down the road?" Obama responded "Well obviously there's a big difference between these two, so" deferring the question while deftly downplaying the fever pitch the campaigns had reached on the eve of potentially defining party primaries.

Perhaps most telling was his willingness to turn the humor upon himself, as he made light of his role as a father and a husband while taking a conciliatory tone towards Clinton. When commenting upon television content and the need for parents to monitor what their children watch, he quipped, "Now, right now, my daughters are mostly on Nickelodeon" and "they know how to work that remote." These comments appeared to establish his credibility as a father and a husband by trotting out well-worn tropes of his lack of control over both his daughters and his wife, self-deprecatory humor that signaled his willingness to admit this and at the same time strengthen his connection with the audience that shared similar experiences with their spouses and offspring.

When Hillary Clinton was asked about her controversial husband, she attempted to deflect the question by exclaiming "he has a spouse too" leading to Obama commenting, "Thankfully Michelle is not on stage. I'm sure she could tell some stories as well." Here, he not only offered a metaphorical olive branch to Clinton after taking heat for his "disrespectful" attitude towards her during their New Hampshire debate and a campaign that had become overheated, he also inoculated himself against attacks upon his past.

The nonverbal behavior of Barack Obama

In comparison with Hillary Clinton, Barack Obama engaged in solo laugher a relatively meager four times. In addition to there being a quantitative difference, there was a qualitative difference in who he laughed at, and why. Although he laughed at a comment by moderator Scott Spradling concerning revving up the Republican attack machine, Obama laughed at his own comments three of the four times he laughed alone. The first time appeared to be a rebuke of Clinton who, during the New Hampshire debate, characterized Obama as being inconsistent on his position on health care. The second time, he took a shot at Clinton during the Super Tuesday debate, commenting about his purported lack of experience, "A lot of Americans disagree," adding that there was support for new leadership. Later that same debate, Obama lampooned Mitt Romney's business skills when he remarked about Romney's continued spending of his own money on what was becoming a highly apparent losing proposition.

Obama's facial display behavior immediately after he made a humorous comment tended toward the deadpan, as he did not smile in over three-quarters of his humorous comments. However, the times he did smile tended to be felt smiles. Furthermore, in three of the five times he did smile, he engaged in solo laughter, as noted above. The other two times he smiled, with both of them felt smiles, occurred during the Super Tuesday debate, with the first time being in response to his wife being able to tell "stories" about him, and the second time being in response to a joint ticket with Hillary Clinton. In other words, his facial behavior tended to mitigate and soften his humorous comments.

John McCain

John McCain's humor is a well-known commodity, serving him well as he played the role of outsider. Coming to the forefront during the 2000 Republican primaries when he and George W. Bush duked it out for the presidential nomination, McCain's humor reflects his temperament, which in turn has been characterized by Baruch College's David S. Birdsell as tending towards being "irascible and pugnacious and clearly stoked by personal animosity"[16] when engaging in the direct confrontations he relishes.[17] However, this willingness to engage in aggressive humor that verged on sarcasm likely drove his maverick persona in which he was a candidate "capable of defying his party or embracing it; holding a worldview that defied any easy ideological setting; having an ironic detachment as he observed himself on the campaign trail, combined with a sly sense of humor that leavened his occasional bursts of temper."[18] In essence, McCain's humor may be seen as reflecting the strengths and weaknesses of his personality, chiefly his ability to see incongruities in himself and others and an aggression that drove his commentary.

The 2008 primary campaign was no exception, as McCain effectively utilized humor to drive home his points. His aggressive form of humor was seen especially in the latter stages of the campaign, namely the New Hampshire and Super Tuesday debates when McCain confronted his fellow contenders, who were most often fellow front-runners challenging his ascendency. However, his first three debate performances were relatively devoid of the biting wit that had come to be associated with McCain.

In the first three Republican presidential primary debates McCain tended to focus the emphasis of his prepared humor on criticizing Congress. Specifically, McCain made light of Congressional approval ratings, stating "And the reason why congressional approval ratings, I saw, at twenty eight percent is, and you get down to blood relatives and paid staffers when you get down that low." Here, interestingly, he was able to mock the same institution that he had been a part of for over a quarter century. His ability to do so without cries of hypocrisy was likely due to the credentials he held as the maverick outsider of that institution, one who was willing to attack colleagues regardless of party, but also one who was willing to work across the aisle.

McCain was not resistant to recycling his humor. He used the same joke twice in the first and second debates to mock Congressional spending, saying "We spent money like a drunken sailor, although I've never known a sailor, drunk or sober, with the imagination of my colleagues" eliciting audience laughter before he went on with the follow up punch-line, saying "and by the way, I received an email recently from a guy who said 'ah, as a former drunken sailor I resent being compared to members of congress.'" Here McCain was able to signal multiple characteristics in this highly encrypted comment. First, he most obviously attacked an unpopular institution, Congress, in turn distancing himself from it. Second, he posited his fiscal conservativism. Finally, he reminded the audience of his Navy service ever-so-subtly.

The other uses of humor by John McCain that elicited audience laughter tended towards the assertive. For instance, when he was queried about California Governor Arnold Schwarzenegger being made eligible to be president, in which case McCain commented "depends on whether he endorses me or not." Likewise, McCain responded to questioning concerning his policy views, stating "And if someone has a better idea, I'd love to have them give it to us."

The one time McCain directly confronted a fellow front-running candidate, Rudy Giuliani, during the second debate, he made reference to the New York mayor's changing political positions, noting "I have kept a consistent position on, ah, right to life and I haven't changed even, ah, on even-numbered years, or have changed because of the different offices that I may be running for." His charges of flip-flopping aimed at his closest competitor at the time, Rudy Giuliani, were later to be reprised in his attacks on his other competition, Mitt Romney. However, the relative dearth of attacks on Giuliani and the reticence seen in McCain's speech qualifiers in this one instance indicates McCain was reluctant to attack his well-documented friend.

There were no dampeners or qualifiers on McCain's attacks on Mitt Romney, the other front-runner. During the New Hampshire debate, McCain made copious use of witticisms that appear to have been off the cuff. While he did make self-deprecating comments concerning his trying to get votes from South Carolina and Iowa, he tended to focus his wit on Romney. Specifically, when Romney came to the defense of drug companies, saying "Don't turn, don't turn the pharmaceutical companies into the big bad guys." McCain responded succinctly, "well, they are" drawing audience laughter. He later revisited the flip-flop charge, stating "when you change your issues, from time to time you will get misquoted." Later in the same debate, he mock agreed with Romney saying, "Governor Romney, we ah, disagree on a lot of issues but I agree you are the candidate of change" drawing laughter from the audience.

However, it was the Super Tuesday debate where McCain truly unleashed his acerbic wit, with nearly half of the comments eliciting laughter attacking Romney, his closest competitor. A number of these attacks involved McCain laughing at Romney for raising taxes, for not having conservative support, even from Romney's former lieutenant governor, and for his business practices. In addition, McCain laughed at Romney when the latter man stated, concerning unsubstantiated claims made by McCain during the New Hampshire debate that Romney flip-flopped on his position concerning the Iraq War surge, "there's not a single media source that I've seen that hasn't said it was reprehensible, even the, even the New York Times said it was wrong" to which McCain responded "Oh" and laughed. Here McCain brushed aside charges concerning dirty politics, laughing off Romney's unease.

The nonverbal behavior of John McCain

If there is one word to describe John McCain's nonverbal behavior, it would be "leaky," as his oftentimes strong emotions would emerge through not just his words, but also his nonverbal actions. Overall, McCain had the greatest variability in the distribution of his facial display behavior (see Table 6.1). While he had the greatest proportion of felt smiles in comparison with Clinton, Huckabee and Obama, he also had the greatest proportion of fear smiles, although these displays may be seen as dominance behavior when eye orientation is taken into account.

Although McCain's solo laughter only erupted during the latter debates, specifically during the New Hampshire and Super Tuesday debates, as thirteen of his fourteen unaccompanied laughs occurred in these latter two debates, these laughs occurred as a result of jibes taken at Mitt Romney or in response to Romney's comments. The acrimony McCain held toward Romney was apparent not just in his humorous comments and the laughter punctuating them, but also in McCain's facial displays. In the majority of his digs at Romney, McCain's eye orientation were coded as staring while his mouth corners were coded as pulled back, often with teeth showing. This is classic threat behavior, and one that is often seen between competing animals when they make dominance displays.[19]

While McCain's display behavior was punctuated by anger-threat towards his closest competitor, Mitt Romney, McCain often would leak his emotions in a variety of forms. In the first debate, he made a harsh pronouncement concerning Osama bin Laden, "We will do whatever is necessary, we will track him down, we will capture, we will bring to justice, and I will follow him to the gates of hell." However, along with these strong words came an awkward "felt smile"

that detracted from his intent. In addition, McCain made what may be best characterized as a "funny face" in response to confusion over who was supposed to
answer a moderator question, with his head dipping down and his face con-
torted.

However, the most telling of McCain's nonverbal displays was an apparently non-conscious response to an innocuous question concerning providing incentives for keeping health care costs down. Here, when he mentioned the efforts of
South Carolina and its Attorney General to keep medical costs down, presumably mocking himself and his attempts to curry votes from the state by highlighting his connections with it, he subtly produced a middle finger, the single digit
renowned for indicating distaste. While he presumably was referring to his connections and the backing he was receiving there during the 2008 primaries,
McCain might also have emotionally responded to his history with the state. In
2000, Karl Rove, mastermind of George W. Bush's presidential campaign,
thwarted McCain's presidential ambitions with a brutal push-poll in which voters were asked whether they "would be more or less likely to vote for John
McCain... if you knew he had fathered an illegitimate black child?" Here, the
Bush campaign, with the help of former State Attorney General Charlie Condon,
smeared McCain and his family by making a racist attack on his adopted then
eight-year-old Bangladeshi daughter, Bridget, who has dark skin. Not only was
this attack highly personal and injurious, it also stopped the momentum McCain
had established in the wake of his 2000 primary victory in New Hampshire.[20] In
sum, McCain might very well have been leaking his personal distaste for his
experience with the state, and the fact that he hired Condon, an architect of the
malicious 2000 attacks, to run his campaign.

Mike Huckabee

Of all the candidates, whether Republican or Democratic, Mike Huckabee was
the one who made the best use of humor to vault himself from long-shot to serious candidate. Although Huckabee's off-handed humor at times landed him in
hot water, such as when he referred to his home state of Arkansas as a "banana
republic," his humor elicited audience laughter and national recognition during
the 2008 presidential primaries. Not only was he considered the funniest Republican candidate by pundits,[21] he earned the title of "Washington, DC's Funniest
Celebrity" as a result of his humor on the campaign trail and during the primary
debates.[22] Using a mix of prepared and spontaneous humor that was in turns
self-deprecatory and attacked presidential candidates on both sides of the aisle,
Huckabee proved himself adept at eliciting audience laughter.

During the first three Republican primary debates, Huckabee leveraged his
humor to obtain greater coverage despite his receiving a lower proportion of
speaking time. He was also able to define himself as a homespun populist with
witticisms, prepared or not, that made reference to his Arkansas roots while he
responded to moderator questions. Specifically, when asked how he would grade
the Bush Administration, he responded: "My teachers never did, I don't know
where you went to school, but in Arkansas we didn't get a grade until it was

over and usually we, ah, didn't want to take it home." However, his down-home humor tended to have a partisan edge as he took the opportunity to contrast himself with the state's two other famous citizens. Upon introducing himself at the beginning of the third debate, he quipped "I'm Mike Huckabee, for ten and a half years I was governor of Arkansas. I'm from, ah, the small town of Hope. You may of heard of it. All I ask is give us one more chance." And when responding to a question concerning Hillary Clinton, he noted "No one on this stage probably knows Hillary Clinton better than I do and I will tell you it is probably not a good idea to have either of them in the White House."

Huckabee did not solely focus his humorous attacks on the Clintons; in two occurrences Huckabee elicited solo laughter from fellow Republican candidate Mitt Romney when he attacked Romney's positions. However, the "game-changing" moment for Huckabee came when he attacked Democratic presidential candidate John Edwards for a campaign gaffe concerning an expensive haircut. Here, Huckabee elicited audience laughter when he commented "We've had a Congress that spent money like John Edwards at a beauty shop."

His ability to poke fun at himself was apparent during the first three debates, as he made fun of his ambitions when, during the first debate, he was asked by the moderator as to whether naturalized citizens such as California Governor Arnold Schwarzenegger should be able to serve as President, commenting "(A)fter I've served eight years as President I'd be happy to change the Constitution for Governor Schwarzenegger." Huckabee made light of his also-ran status during the second debate when he noted in response to a moniker making fun of the top-three candidates ("Rudy McRomney") that "well, it's a form of flattery to be attacked, but ah, I wish my name would get in the moniker that Governor Gilmore's putting out there I, I could use the bump." He also took a dig at his status as a Southern Baptist preacher and his presumed status as religious arbiter when asked a moral question, stating "Well, it looks like I'm getting all the moral questions tonight and I guess that's a good thing," before further commenting "That's better than getting the immoral questions (laughter), so I'm happy to get those."

Although his production of humor diminished significantly during the New Hampshire debate, as he appeared perturbed by the lack of speaking time, Huckabee was able to ridicule Romney's position on the Iraq War and surge in troops, portraying him as changing positions by quipping "which one?" and joke about the cost of health care noting, "it's about a thousand dollars for a Kleenex in a hospital anymore." However, Huckabee was able to use humor to greater effect in the Super Tuesday debate, albeit using a familiar strategy of self-deprecation in reference to Republican icons Rush Limbaugh ("You know, I wish Rush loved me as much as I love Rush") and Ronald Reagan. In this latter case, when asked about Reagan's legacy, specifically in reference to his selection of pro-choice Supreme Court justice Sandra Day O'Connor, Huckabee demurred by quipping, "History will have to determine that, and I'm not gonna come to the Reagan library and say anything about Ronald Reagan's decisions; I'm not that stupid, if I was I'd have no business being President." Here Huckabee deftly sidestepped a "gotcha" question that would pit him against either the policy preferences of his pro-life support or the larger-than-life legacy of Republican Party icon Ronald Reagan.

While Huckabee yet again used humor to lament his lack of speaking time during the Super Tuesday debate in comparison with combative front-runners McCain and Romney, commenting "Well first of all, I didn't come here to umpire a ballgame between (these) two," his finest moment during the debate came as a result of what appeared to be prepared humorous comments that self-deprecatingly referred to his political ambitions. Here, Huckabee engaged in observational humor concerning the policy of investing in public infrastructure to reduce the commuting time of the average American by commenting, "That's a full work week, not on vacation, not spent with their kids, stuck in traffic, just sitting there behind the wheel pointing fingers usually one at a time, at other motorists, and (laughter) very upset with what's going on around them in traffic" before making light of himself, pointing out "Now, my point is, it is not necessarily just I-95 from Bangor to Miami, I said that when I was in Florida; today we might look at a Western highway that would go down the Californian coast." With the likely prepared humorous comment Huckabee was able to connect with the average American's exasperation with long commutes and wasted time, but at the same time was able to make fun of his electoral ambitions.

The nonverbal behavior of Mike Huckabee

Interestingly, or maybe not so much given Mike Huckabee's joke telling abilities, was his complete lack of smiling at his own humorous comments. Indeed if there is one quality that defines the great majority of Huckabee's nonverbal cues, it is his deadpan face when delivering his humorous comments. Of the twenty-three laughter eliciting comments made by Huckabee, 95 percent of those code-able events did not involve him displaying a smile (see Table 6.1). Specifically, while his lower face, namely his mouth corners remain normal and he tended not to show his teeth, his highly expressive eyebrows tended to elevate in either affected shock or surprise or lower and furrow in mock consternation, punctuating Huckabee's delivery with nonverbal exclamation points. The one time he did display a smile, in this case a fear smile, it was after he commented about his roots in Hope, Arkansas, in which he signaled mock fear concerning his connection with fellow hometown boy, ex-President Bill Clinton. However, what stands out is his maintaining eye contact immediately following his humorous comments, with a "staring" eye orientation occurring in 70 percent of the cases coded, indicating dominance behavior.

Conclusions

Although primary elections are typically seen as the province of the politically attentive public, and as a result are more likely to feature encrypted humor that only political junkies would understand and appreciate,[2, 3] the 2008 election drew much greater interest from a broader public. This was due to a confluence of factors, including the scope of candidates and the range of their characteristics, which included a Mormon, a Latino, an African American, a woman, and the eldest candidate to date, as well as number of highly politically salient issues including two wars and a failing economy. Each of these candidates attempted to portray themselves as supporting the values of their political party by displaying their personality traits in their verbal response, particularly through the humor they used.

The use of encrypted humor, in which the humorous comment was crafted to subtly summon images available only to those "in the know" occurred relatively rarely. When encrypted humorous comments did occur, with John McCain's "Congress spending money like a drunken sailor" remark or Mike Huckabee's "John Edwards in a beauty shop" comment, they were in the early stages of the campaign when die-hard political junkies were likely to pay close attention and then financially support those candidates who stood out. Likewise, the single time Barack Obama used what appeared to be a prepared humor with an "encrypted" element came before the PBS debate when there was a predominantly African American audience who would appreciate the in-group element of the comment. That the occurrence of encrypted humor tailed off during the latter debates, when votes mattered more than financial support, suggests and appreciation for a more broadly focused campaign strategy inclusive of more than just die-hard partisans.

That does not mean that personality traits and political values held dear by partisan voters were not accentuated. Indeed, the humor of the candidates reflected the values of the parties' rank-and-file, and when it did not, the candidate suffered. Obama's response to Clinton's New Hampshire "likeability" moment made him appear unconscientious and disagreeable, contrary to the personality traits valued by Democratic Party identifiers. This in turn hurt his position and appeared to affect the type of humor both Obama and Clinton used in the Super Tuesday debate. Here, neither candidate went for the jugular of their opponent with their humorous comments, saving their most acerbic comments for the incumbent President George W. Bush. Indeed, their humorous comments were amicable, and their nonverbal behavior was marked by mostly felt smiles in response to the opposing candidate.

The emphasis of John McCain's humorous comments was on attacking fellow front-runner Mitt Romney. Here, McCain tarred Romney as a flip-flopper willing to change positions on any policy issue in order to attain the presidency. In the words of Kevin Smith et al.[9] McCain played upon the need for successful party members "to stand ready not only to elevate and obey leaders but also keep an unblinking eye on those leaders and to be prepared to cut them down to size if they act in a self-serving fashion or seem to believe they deserve special treatment" (p. 286). These types of attacks likely resonated more with the Republican Party base due to their preference for strong leaders who would stay true to their stated values.

While Huckabee did not engage in this manner of aggressive attacks verbally, his nonverbal behavior provided evidence of someone who "would not blink" and would not betray emotions, especially in the lower part of his face. These behaviors, as discussed extensively in chapter 5, are indicative of a dominant-agonic leadership style. Taken in conjunction with his willingness to make light of his political aspirations, Huckabee was able to establish himself as leadership material through his words and actions, while at the same time avoiding aggressive actions against specific Republican candidates.

On the other hand, the Democratic Party front-runners did not display the level of aggression seen in their Republican counterparts. Barack Obama, while not smiling in the wake of most of his humorous comments, focused then cut off eye contact, avoiding stare-downs. Hillary Clinton showed similar nonverbal behavior in terms of eye contact; however, more importantly she displayed a range of smiles, engaging in a much more varied pattern of emotional communication. Whether this was due to a general desire by both candidates to be polite[10] or a fear of treading in dangerous territory of humor that may easily be inferred or spun as being racist or sexist for an audience highly attenuated to such threats to conscientiousness is not known; what is known is that the sharpness of the humor, and attendant nonverbal displays, used by the Clinton and Obama pales in comparison with that of the Republicans studied here.

In sum, while the analysis employed here is exploratory and makes conclusions based upon a limited database of four presidential candidates engaging in ten primary debates, the results suggest humorous comments and the displays accompanying them do more than signal intelligence by the candidates either being able to match a prepared comment with an appropriate moment or being able to manufacture wit on the spot, it also signals the norms and personality traits valued by their partisan base of voters. Although highly encrypted humor did not occur often enough to differentiate which group a candidate was targeting his or her comments at, there was more than enough variance in the humor styles of the four candidates to attribute specific personality traits to each and allow voters to sort themselves into camps of followers.

Notes

[a] It might be argued that those individuals who are more socially attuned, and thus more likely to respond with laughter, are those who are more trusting and generous.

[b] A further insult was seen in the question itself, with women noting the question "wouldn't be coming up if she wasn't a woman" (Kantor 2008: A-22).

[c] This exchange may be seen as especially fraught with meaning in light of President Bill Clinton's sex-scandal with Monica Lewinsky and the inferred point that Hillary Clinton could not control her husband then, and still did not have him under control—a comment that likely could not have been made by a man.

[d] Alternative interpretations of the use of honorifics such as "Senator" to refer to Hillary Clinton see this as a subtle way of stressing her political insider status, or even as a way of distancing and separating her from a more convivial "boys' club."

References

1. Morreall, J. in *Comic relief: A comprehensive philosophy of humor* 187 (Wiley-Blackwell, Malden, MA, 2009).
2. Flamson, T. & Barrett, H. C. The encryption theory of humor: A knowledge-based mechanism of honest signaling. *Journal of Evolutionary Psychology* 6, 261-281 (2008).
3. Flamson, T. The encryption theory: Studies in Brazil and the United States testing an evolutionary explanation of humor as an honest signal. University of California, Las Angeles, CA, 1-167 (2010).
4. Weisfeld, G. E. The adaptive value of humor and laughter. *Ethology & Sociobiology 14*, 141-169 (1993).
5. Alexander, R. Ostracism and Indirect Reciprocity: The Reproductive Significance of Humor. *Ethology and Sociobiology 7* (1986).
6. Platow, M. J. *et al.* "It's not funny if they're laughing": Self-categorization, social influence, and responses to canned laughter. *J. Exp. Soc. Psychol. 41*, 542-550 (2005).
7. Miller, G. F. in *The mating mind: How sexual choice shaped the evolution of human nature* (Doubleday Books, New York, NY, 2000).
8. Greengross, G. & Miller, G. F. Dissing oneself versus dissing rivals: Effects of status, personality, and sex on the short-term and long-term attractiveness of self-deprecating and other-deprecating humor. *Evolutionary Psychology* 6, 393-408 (2008).
9. Smith, K. B., Larimer, C. W., Littvay, L. & Hibbing, J. R. Evolutionary theory and political leadership: Why certain people do not trust decision makers. *The Journal of Politics 69*, 285-299 (2007).
10. Dailey, W. O., Hinck, E. A. & Hinck, S. S. Audience Perceptions of Politeness and Advocacy Skills in the 2000 and 2004 Presidential Debates. *Argumentation and Advocacy 41*, 196-210 (2005).
11. Hillygus, D. S. & Shields, T. G. in *The persuadable voter: Wedge issues in presidential campaigns* (Princeton University Press, Princeton, NJ, 2009).
12. Kantor, J. Sexism involving Clinton rankles certain sizable demographic. *New York Times* A, 22 (2008).
13. Grabe, M. E. & Bucy, E. P. in *Image bite politics: news and the visual framing of elections* 316 (Oxford University Press, Oxford; New York, 2009).
14. Kurtz, H. Hillary chuckles; Pundits snort: Clinton's robust yuks lead to analysis of appeal of laughter. *Washington Post* C, 1 (2007).
15. Gutgold, N. D. in *Almost Madam President: Why Hillary Clinton "won" in 2008* 119 (Lexington Books, New York, 2009).
16. Seelye, K. Q. A scrappy fighter, with a debating style honed in and out of politics. *New York Times* A, 25 (2008).
17. Leahy, M. McCain: A question of temperament. *Washington Post* A, 1 (2008).

18. Nagourney, A. & Santora, M. Terror Attack Scenario Exposes Deep Differences Among G.O.P. Hopefuls. *New York Times* Politics (2007).
19. Darwin, C., Ekman, P. & Prodger, P. in *The expression of the emotions in man and animals* (Oxford University Press, New York, NY, 2002).
20. Banks, A. Dirty tricks, South Carolina and John McCain. *The Nation* (2010).
21. McFeatters, A. Candidates know value of a laugh. *Seattle Post Intellegencer* G, 2 (2007).
22. Sadler, A. Huckabee crowned "funniest celebrity." *The Morning News* B, 8 (2008).

Chapter 7
Playful Politicians:
Why Laughter and Humor Matters in the
Rough-and-Tumble World of Politics

The bulk of this book has been spent systematically analyzing the use of humor in the 2008 presidential primary debates. While this election proved to be an exceptional one, not the least for its diversity of candidate characteristics, it provided a rare opportunity to consider similarities and differences between the political parties and the role laughter and humor plays. Although the first two chapters focused on what has been written before concerning humor as used by politicians to portray themselves, and posited a model drawing upon the latest multi-disciplinary research based upon evolutionary theory both as to the why and how of humor, I believe the most important contribution this book makes is the systematic observational analysis of the humor that occurred during these debates. Specifically, the pain-staking, in-depth and rigorous analysis of the data collected from five Republican and five Democratic Party debates allows for conclusions to be drawn, suggestions to be made, and future research to be considered.

There has been a great deal of concern expressed through the years over the lack of knowledge the average citizen has regarding politics and policy and how this leads to faulty choices in political leaders[1] and concomitantly how this reflects poorly on a mass media more caught up in horse race coverage and the ever-diminishing sound and visual bites.[2] While there are certainly reasons to be concerned about an ill- or un-informed electorate and the print and electronic media not covering the substance of politics and policy, the choice of leaders on the basis of limited information is not necessarily a fatal concern for representative government. Debates, while critiqued as side-by-side press conferences, and often structured to attempt to mask candidate shortcomings, are despite the framing beforehand and the spin afterwards, the best unmediated means by which a citizen may acquire information about candidates for leadership. In other words, debates provide the opportunity for "thin-slice" judgments to be made, quick assessments of personal qualities that have been shown to be accurate despite limited processing and time.[3]

That primary debates provide a popular means by which contenders may be separated from the pretenders is borne out by the forty primary debates during the 2008 presidential primary electoral season. While the early debates set the initial tone for the presidential campaign, and the debates prior to the primary elections themselves set the stage for the vote, each debate provided candidates with the opportunity to shine or stumble, all recorded for posterity. It is here where humor, and the audience laughter signaling successful attempts at it, becomes important as it provides candidates the opportunity to shine by connecting with the audience, and at the same time conveys information about the candidate's intelligence, values, and personality both verbally and nonverbally. This is perhaps most important for candidates who are not already known by voters, and who need an entry point into the hearts and minds of the public and mass media.

Perhaps the most immediately pertinent information this book provides is found in chapter 3, where we consider dominance of attention and the use of humor to attain it. The first finding is that there is not a level playing field when it comes to the initial six presidential primary debate—a time when it would be most expected that the candidates would have relatively equal time and attention. Specifically, it appears the front-runners were already chosen by partisans through their financial gifts, and by the mass media, whether print or electronic, through the coverage they received. Perhaps more important, when one considers the role of debates as the one opportunity where voters get an un-mediated taste of the candidates, there was a significant dominance of attention by the front-runners in these early debates. It is in this context that humor becomes important as a tool for obtaining attention, as the print media is more likely to give coverage to candidates who elicited more audience laughter. However, as humor does not appear to affect financial gifts or the electronic media, a position as front-runner is self-perpetuating and hard to break into. That does not mean a successful humorous comment—a home run witticism—cannot play the role of game changer. Indeed, there is some evidence to suggest Mike Huckabee's media profile shifted radically due to one particular comment about John Edwards, a beauty shop, and Congressional spending. Statistically, however, evidence for more humor equaling more coverage and financial sustenance is not found.

Humor, despite its ephemeral nature, is still omnipresent during the debates studied here. Breaking it down into component parts for more systematic analysis forms the basis for the next three chapters of the book. Specifically, John Morreall's approach to humor proved useful in informing the analysis undertaken in this book, especially when working backward from the laughter signaling pleasure (chapter 4) to the signaling of the play mode, or more accurately, the comment maker's intent through facial display behavior (chapter 5) to, finally, the starting point of the rapid cognitive shift in thoughts or perceptions that started the entire humor process, albeit with a focus on the "exceptional" primary candidates (chapter 6). Regrettably, the data available does not allow for the analysis of either failed humor or humor that was amusing, yet did not elicit laughter. While there are certainly instances of laughter due to misstatements, such as when Joe Biden's saying "(G)etting people in the position where testing matters. I got tested for AIDS, I know Barack got tested for AIDS (laughter). There's no shame in getting tested for AIDS" led the audience to infer he was claiming a personal relationship with Obama, or due to the lack of connection with reality, such as when moderator Charles Gibson claimed "(I)f you take a family, if you take a family of two professors here at St. Anselm they're going to be in the $200,000 category that you're talking about lifting on . . ." to which the audience laughed and Barack Obama stated "I don't think they agree with you", these are relatively rare.

The first step in the process of understanding the influence of humor is to look at the occurrence of laughter, the source of the comment, and the target of the witticism. Laughter that is elicited by humorous comments tends to come at the expense of the opposition, whether they are immediate competition or the out-group. Furthermore, despite more opportunities in terms of debate time for front-runners, humor tends to be used by the underdog candidates. Here, the experience of Republican candidates Mike Huckabee and John McCain is instructive as both candidates using different types of humor (chapter 6) energized their campaigns and mobilized support, in essence using humor to level the playing field.

Vocalic and verbal attributes are only part of the picture; nonverbal displays signaled via the face in the wake of humor punctuate these comments and communicates intent. That facial display behavior plays a role in the delivery and reception of humor is no surprise, especially as there is a long and storied appreciation for the nonverbal attributes of charisma that dates back to at least the first Nixon-Kennedy debate, if not before. The influence of different configurations of the eyes and the mouth concurrent with humorous comments, especially in the more predominant affiliative smile displays of happiness-reassurance, can be seen in both who laughed at the comments and how hard the audience laughed. While preliminary, perhaps the most important finding is that a smile is not just a smile, but can convey a multitude of meanings depending on its configuration.

Although I focus solely on the four most successful candidates for both parties in considering the humorous utterances themselves and the personal values and style they communicate, I find much to differentiate the candidates based upon their values and personality. Each brought a different style in terms of humor produced and nonverbal display behavior. While Hillary Clinton was able to alter perceptions of herself through self-deprecating humor, the story surrounding her laugh—the "Clinton Cackle"—rose to unexpected prominence, especially given the defensive laughing tactics of fellow front-runner Mitt Romney. Meanwhile, the story of Barack Obama was one of good natured humor that occurred quite often despite the public perception of a detached and cerebral candidate.

While the Democratic Party candidates provide a prime example of humor tending towards the self-deprecatory and relatively inoffensive, the Republican Party candidates provide an altogether different story. Both Mike Huckabee and John McCain appeared to use humor like underdogs, with their biting wit focused on direct competitors (in McCain's case, predominantly Mitt Romney) or the out-group. While both appeared to use humor aggressively and effectively, nonverbally McCain tended to leak his emotions most. On the other hand,

Huckabee was able to use humor in an amiable manner, although his facial display behavior can be seen as tending towards agonic-dominance, with very few
smiles and more often than not, him holding a stare. Huckabee was also the candidate who was able to use humor the most effectively, vaulting himself from
the pack to front-runner despite a relative lack of organization and financial support.

Finally, while this book does not directly test the evolutionary theories it
draws from, the evidence seen in the ten presidential primary debates provides
support for using this unifying perspective and proffers insight as to how humor
and laughter might benefit individuals and groups in political, indeed, social
situations. Namely I concur with Gervais and Sloan-Wilson[4] when they state
"(W)e argue that the benefits incurred through laughter and play often occur at
the group level as well as at the individual level, and between group selection
could thus have played a significant role in the elaboration of laughter and humor in humans" (p. 410). Therefore, while Flamson and Barrett's[5] encryption
theory of humor, which posits that humor helps individuals sort into successful
groups through shared values, experiences and personality by indexing these
qualities, provides the most advanced and powerful approach to understanding
political humor, humor also preferentially advances the prestige of candidates[6]
who use it to successfully elicit audience laughter, as well as presumably their
reproductive success, although this is not tested.

Suggestions

Political strategists would do well to pay attention to humor and its use during
presidential debates. The American public has shown an appreciation for quick-
witted presidents who are able to make a humorous comment during appropriate
moments or make a clever rejoinder, with John F. Kennedy and Ronald Reagan
in the pantheon of presidents revered for their charisma regardless of their political accomplishments. Furthermore, while the mass media may not appreciate
the un-mediated environment provided by debates, they appreciate a powerful
sound bite, providing more coverage in response. On the other hand, campaign
gaffes, such as a humorous comment that offends, insults or falls flat, are likewise covered to a greater extent.[7] In other words, campaigns should be aware of
not just the benefits of successful humor, but also the potential pitfalls when
humor fails.

This is especially the case in primary races where multiple debates present
wars of attrition when compared to the general election, where knockout blows
can be scored in front of the cameras and replayed in the print and electronic
press, as well as the internet. Because these moments are so sound- and image-
bite worthy,[2] they are almost assured of continued airplay in the twenty-four-
hour cable news cycle, although the likelihood that such comments will be analyzed and critiqued by the media is diminished.[8] Furthermore, there is no doubt
such comments are memorable and will lead to further discussion amongst individuals,[9, 10] although critical scrutiny likely will be lacking.[10, 11]

In conclusion, humor as exercised by, and even against, political candidates
during the televised era, in which there is a virtual face-to-face interaction be-

tween the candidates and the voting public, can humanize candidates,[12] even leading to increased campaign contributions.[13] Humor can likewise backfire if it is used inappropriately or if it is seen as absent in a candidate.[14] Examples of backfiring humor, even when candidates are caught using it "off-camera," are instructive. For instance, Thomas Patterson recounting of how Nebraska Senator and presidential aspirant Bob Kerrey making a joke about lesbians in New Hampshire during the 1992 primary election became big news and harmed his electoral chances[7] (p. 148) recapitulates Morris Udall's admonitions to avoid racist, ethnic and sexist jokes.[15] In any case, the use of humor as a strategy to both draw attention to the candidate, signaling their qualities as a leader, and pithily asserting positions can be expected, especially in light of the growing evidence underscoring the power of late night humor to frame candidate qualities for the public.

Future research

Although this book has answered a great many questions concerning the use of humor and the resulting laughter in presidential primary debates, it still leaves a great many questions unresolved. These questions may be seen at each stage of the "basic pattern of humor" and may be seen as important for understanding not just humor in the political arena, but how humor is used in the daily lives of individuals. And as has been seen here, decomposing humor into its elements has led to fruitful analysis; further fine-tuning the analysis of humor components will likely lead to more accurate assertions and better insights into human behavior.

Questions concerning laughter might consider what information it provides beyond just who laughs, how hard, and how long, and address issues in the political arena to a greater extent. For example, research by Szameitat et al.[16] found that joyous, taunting, schadenfreude and tickle laughter coming from individuals may be differentiated by listeners. This leads to the question of whether audience laughter can signal such information. Systematic testing of how listeners code laughter, and whether they can discriminate between humor that excludes others by taunting the target, or solidifies personal connections through shared joyous feelings, would do much to help us understand the role laughter plays in political gatherings.

Furthermore, as has been seen in our analysis of individual candidates laughing, both Mitt Romney and Hillary Clinton (with the media named "Clinton Cackle") engaged in highly loud and identifiable solo laughter in response to attacks on them. Can such laughter signal dominance by making the candidate easily identifiable, and if it is indeed used to laugh off attacks, how does it function?

Future research should consider nonverbal display behavior more closely. While this study has advanced our understanding of different types of display behavior by moving beyond the gestalt approach to coding facial displays, more precise analysis through such coding instruments as the Facial Action Coding System (FACS), while time consuming, provide a tool to consider what components of facial displays play the most relevant role in communicating humorous intent. In other words, does the sight of a candidate laughing, whether with the prototypical play face displaying a loose jaw, exposed upper teeth, and narrowed eyes, or a more aggressive taunting laughter (as may be the case with solo laughter by candidates in response to attacks) influence the attitudes of viewers? And if so, what are the key components—the facial display or the vocalic qualities of the laugh itself?

Questions concerning humor are much more involved, due to humorous comments involving a sequence of events, and a range of theories that operate at multiple different levels. For instance, on a strategic level of analysis, does laughter as a result of a candidate's humorous comments tend to occur at different times of the debate, and does this timing issue lead to different perceptions by viewers. And what is the relationship between humor and candidate likability? Do candidates become more likeable as a result of making a humorous comment? And does it matter what type of humorous comment is made, whether self- or other-deprecatory? Furthermore, do politicians become more "funny" when they win, with higher status ascribing a halo of humorousness?

The type of humor, whether highly encrypted or not, is also of interest. Flamson and Barrett[5] have shown that encrypted humor is deemed funnier and as a result appreciated to a greater extent by individuals with "insider" knowledge available to decode the incongruity of what might otherwise be an obscure comment. Looking beyond debates to political events, will candidates who can use encrypted humor be given the "keys" to the hearts and minds of partisans? Specifically, more highly encrypted humor occurred early in the primary debates when strong partisans were more likely to be interested in candidate selection and support, both through financial sources and through volunteering efforts, suggesting a shared language that might exclude others is an acceptable strategy that might be seen during gatherings of supporters. That highly encrypted humor did not occur later on during the New Hampshire and Super Tuesday debates likewise suggests that reaching out to a larger audience without alienating them through obscure humorous comments might be more important, especially given large audiences of voters watching the debates on television where they are not as prone to contagiousness of audience laughter.

Finally, looking more systemically, does the use of humor vary systematically from nation to nation? And is the use of humor the "ultimate" signal of egalitarian values within a society? Egalitarian and individualistic nations such as the United States and Great Britain have a long and illustrious history of humor being used by politicians, both to reduce the profile of others, and increase their own likability. Anecdotally, nations with a growing appreciation for democracy and one-person, one-vote values, such as Russia, are seeing politicians who are much more aware of their media-profile and the need to make themselves more likable, often through a range of photo opportunities as well as through self-deprecatory humor.

Parting thoughts

Although humor is typically considered light-hearted and pro-social, it has what may be considered a "darker" side. As we have seen, it may be used to denigrate individuals and groups that are seen as not conforming to standards held by the individuals making the comments and those laughing at those comments. At the same time, by not directly attacking the opposition, humor is not necessarily seen as "impolite" or "rude"[17] especially if the audience laughs. In sum, it is a tool that may be used to strengthen certain individuals and groups at the expense of other individuals and groups. This may be especially the case with politics, in which competing and hostile groups and individuals attempt to form coalitions against each other for control of the "spoils" within a larger encompassing group. In egalitarian democratic societies, such as the United States, political competition does not take the form of actual physical coercive activities, instead it takes on the form of verbal (and nonverbal) competition, with each leaders of coalitions attempting to gain political control through the use of masterful rhetoric and other persuasive strategies to win votes and elections.

However, when candidates substitute crowd- and press-pleasing forays into humor for serious discussion of issues, and when the press not only plays to the entertainment properties of these comments, real concerns may go unaddressed. Knowing how humor is used, and why it is performed, can lead to a more aware electorate and press. As seen here, humor as exercised by presidential candidates in the 2008 primaries played a serious role in enhancing electoral status, and likely will continue to play an important role in making candidates more likeable and hence more electable in future elections.

References
1. Campbell, A., Converse, P. E., Miller, W. E. & Stokes, D. E. in *The American voter* 573 (Wiley, New York, 1960).
2. Grabe, M. E. & Bucy, E. P. in *Image bite politics: news and the visual framing of elections* 316 (Oxford University Press, Oxford; New York, 2009).
3. Borkenau, P., Mauer, N., Riemann, R., Spinath, F. M. & Angleitner, A. Thin slices of behavior as cues of personality and intelligence. *J. Pers. Soc. Psychol.* 86, 599-614 (2004).
4. Gervais, M. & Wilson, D. S. The evolution and functions of laughter and humor: a synthetic approach. *Q. Rev. Biol.* 80, 395-430 (2005).
5. Flamson, T. & Barrett, H. C. The encryption theory of humor: A knowledge-based mechanism of honest signaling. *Journal of Evolutionary Psychology* 6, 261-281 (2008).
6. Henrich, J. & Gil-White, F. J. The evolution of prestige: Freely conferred deference as a mechanism for enhancing the benefits of cultural transmission. *Evolution and Human Behavior* 22, 165-196 (2001).
7. Patterson, T. E. in *Out of Order* (Alfred A. Knopf, New York, 1993).
8. Bennett, W. L. in *News, the politics of illusion* 216 (Longman, New York, 1988).
9. Fein, S., Goethals, G. R. & Kugler, M. B. Social Influence on Political Judgments: The Case of Presidential Debates. *Polit. Psychol.* 28, 165-192 (2007).

10. Nabi, R. L., Moyer-Guseé, E. & Byrne, S. All Joking Aside: A Serious In-
    vestigation into the Persuasive Effect of Funny Social Issue Messages.
    Communication Monographs 74, 29-54 (2007).
11. Young, D. G. The Privileged Role of the Late-Night Joke: Exploring Hu-
    mor's Role in Disrupting Argument Scrutiny. *Media Psychology* 11, 119-
    142 (2008).
12. Baym, G. Representation and the Politics of Play: Stephen Colbert's Better
    Know a District. *Political Communication* 24, 359-376 (2007).
13. Fowler, J. H. The Colbert Bump in Campaign Donations: More Truthful
    than Truthy. *PS: Political Science and Politics* 41, 533-539 (2008).
14. Compton, J. More than laughing? Survey of political humor effects research.
    Laughing matters: Humor and American politics in the media age, 39-66
    (2007).
15. Udall, M. K. in *Too funny to be President* 249 (The University of Arizona
    Press, Tucson, AZ, 1988).
16. Szameitat, D. P. *et al.* Differentiation of emotions in laughter at the beha-
    vioral level. *Emotion* 9, 397-405 (2009).
17. Dailey, W. O., Hinck, E. A. & Hinck, S. S. Audience Perceptions of Polite-
    ness and Advocacy Skills in the 2000 and 2004 Presidential Debates. *Ar-
    gumentation and Advocacy* 41, 196-210 (2005).

Appendix
Inter-Coder Reliability

To ensure reliability, the data were coded by two independent coders. Data for all variables were run using Krippendorff's alpha with the variables set at categorical with a high level of reliability for all variables considered. The choice of inter-coder reliability statistic is based upon Hayes and Krippendorff's argument that a good index should reflect five qualities: 1) assessing agreement from independent coders; 2) should not be confounded by the number of categories or scale points available for coding; 3) should be anchored by two points that are easily interpreted; 4) should be appropriate to the datas' level of measurement; and 5) should have a known or computable sampling behavior.[1] Therefore, Krippendorff's alpha was run using a macro for SPSS.

The target of the humorous comment is coded as focusing on either the speaker him/herself, the speaker's family, the speaker's in-group, the moderator, the audience, a competitor, or finally, the speaker's out-group. Inter-coder reliability for 315 cases was ascertained using Krippendorff's alpha, which exhibited very high levels of agreement (α=.9144). The Krippendorff's alpha of .7696 for the strength of audience laughter is highly reliable, especially given the highly subjective nature of judging laughter strength (Rosenthal, 2005). Nonverbal measurement reliability for each of the five facial display categories considered is high with inter-coder agreement about the eyes over 90 percent for all three categories (eyebrows Krippendorff's α=.9212; eyelids Krippendorff's α=.9104; eye orientation Krippendorff's α=.9414). Likewise, agreement concerning the lower face is strong with the mouth corners (Krippendorff's α=.8604) and teeth showing (Krippendorff's α=.9148) high levels of intercoder agreement.

To further test inter-coder reliability, Cohen's Kappa was run. Findings replicate Krippendorff's Alpha (eyebrows κ=.922; eyelids κ=.920; eye orientation κ=.942; mouth corners κ=.861; teeth showing κ=.915) with high levels of inter-coder reliability across all nonverbal categories.

References

1. Hayes, A. F. & Krippendorff, K. Answering the call for a standard reliability measure for coding data. *Communication Methods and Measures* 1, 77-89 (2007).

Roosevelt, Franklin D., 4
Rove, Karl, 55, 116
Rudy McRomney, 64, 117

S

Sadness-Appeasement, 23, 82, 84,
86, 89, 94, 95
Salter, Frank, 19, 23, 24, 32, 34,
51, 57, 75, 76, 82, 99
Saturday Night Live, 3
Schieffer, Bob, 109
Schwarzenegger, Arnold, 26, 114,
117
second-tier candidates, 9, 44, 46,
59, 63, 64, 65, 66, 67, 68, 69,
93, 94
self-deprecatory, 3, 4, 7, 21, 22,
24, 25, 26, 28, 29, 53, 69, 70,
106, 107, 108, 110, 111, 112,
116, 125, 128
September 11, 2001, 40
sexual selection, 17, 20, 21, 22, 30
signaling theory, 8, 17, 21
Sloane, A. A, 4, 12, 35
Smiley, Tavis, 10, 111
Smith, Kevin, 34, 106, 119, 121
Soviet Union, 2, 16, 23
Spoiler Candidates, 47
Spradling, Scott, 109, 110, 113
Stewart, Jon, 23
Super Tuesday, 1, 7, 10, 55, 59, 62,
63, 69, 108, 110, 111, 113, 115,
117, 118, 119, 128
Superiority Theory of Humor, 5,
72
Szameitat, 32, 75, 127, 130

T

Thorstein & Veblen, 17
Tancredo, Tom, 10, 27, 42, 64, 65,
68
"thin slice," 3, 4, 8, 12, 105, 123,
129
Thompson, Fred, 10, 40, 64, 68,
69, 70,

Thompson, Tommy, 10, 42, 64, 65,
68
totalitarian, 22

U

Udall, Morris K., 3, 11, 12, 34, 127,
130

W

Wall Street Journal, 41
Wallace, Chris, 109
Waller, Cray, and Burrows, 81,
100
Washington Post, 41, 121
White House, 3, 4, 12, 25, 35, 109,
110, 117
Williams, Brian, 10, 58

Y

Yarwood, Dean L., 4, 11, 12, 33, 73

Z

zero-sum, 23